ALFRESCO

ALFRESCO

OVER 100 RECIPES WITH MENUS FOR
MEMORABLE OUTDOOR MEALS

Linda Burgess and Rosamond Richardson

CLARKSON POTTER PUBLISHERS
NEW YORK

Published in the United States of America
by Clarkson N. Potter, Inc.
201 East 50th Street, New York, New York, 10022.
Member of the Crown Publishing Group.

First Published by Ebury Press
an imprint of the Random Century Group
Random Century House
20 Vauxhall Bridge Road
London SW1V 2SA

CLARKSON N. POTTER, POTTER and Colophon are trademarks of
Clarkson N. Potter, Inc.

Manufactured in Italy

Library of Congress Cataloging-in-Publication information is available.

ISBN 0-517-58482-4

Measurements and ingredients

All measurements give the metric amount first, followed in
brackets (parentheses) by the Imperial equivalent, and then the
U.S. equivalent if different. If the Imperial and U.S. equivalents
are the same, only one measurement is given in brackets. As the
equivalents are not exact, please work from one set of figures.
U.S. pints, quarts and gallons are twenty per cent smaller than
Imperial ones.

Unless otherwise specified in the recipes, use freshly ground
black pepper, slightly salted butter, good-quality olive oil,
medium-sized vegetables and size 3 (medium-sized) eggs. In
the United States, if you have difficulty finding superfine sugar,
U.S. granulated sugar may be substituted, as it is finer than
British granulated sugar.

FOREWORD

THE EXPERIENCE of eating summery food in the long grass of a leafy glade, or in the cool shade of a willow by the river, becomes a lifelong memory. The warm sunshine of a beach in early morning, a stream gliding through a meadow at midday, highlight the pleasures of eating alfresco. Different places have their particular appeal: the tranquillity of a green lane, the peace of a distant field, the open space of the hills or mountains. Feel the grass under your bare feet as you unpack the picnic hamper, a slight breeze cooling the skin as you sip chilled fruit punch or iced mint tea, and you are in a different world.

Even eating out in the garden is a completely different experience from a meal indoors. The scents of the season mingle with the enjoyment of delicious food: the heady fragrance of hawthorn blossom in spring, honeysuckle in high summer, roses tumbling over the fence until autumn. Sitting on the lawn, or in a shady orchard, on a patio or in a conservatory or sunporch, alfresco meals make vivid impressions that linger long after the day is over.

Picnics have elements of celebration and spontaneity about them. On those glorious days early in the year, warm and bright with that unique energy which spells spring, the feeling of freedom as you take off to a beautiful spot in the countryside, with lunch packed into a basket, is incomparable. By the time summer comes, with its long days of sunshine, eating alfresco can become more or less habitual. Whether in the garden, by a lake or in the mountains, in woods or a rocky cove by the sea, you can take a picnic with you to enjoy the pleasures of a summer's day in peace. Once the year begins to turn, and stubble fields catch the red-gold of a waning sun, picnics can be combined with traditional countryside expeditions—berrying, nutting, or mushrooming in the woods.

On a patio that catches the early morning sun, it is wonderful to eat breakfast alfresco, absorbing the freshness of the new day as you linger over the meal. Or organize a breakfast picnic the night before: it is a sensational way to start a summer's day.

As the sun travels higher in the sky, and noon becomes breathless in the fierce midday heat, relax in the shade with a long cooling drink. Pack a hamper with epicurean dishes and take to the countryside with a bottle of white wine to cool in a running stream. Explore the fields and footpaths with a picnic basket full of teatime treats.

As evening draws on and the heat of the day diminishes, shadows lengthen over the land and a slight breeze cools the air. It is a lovely time of day to enjoy a glass of chilled fruit cup in the dappled shade of trees on the lawn. Follow this with a light, summery meal on the patio as early evening fades into twilight. On perfect summer nights, have a dinner party at dusk in the garden, candlelit under the stars, enjoying the last vestiges of warmth as dusk merges into darkness. As midsummer dew rises over the land, moon shadows slant across the table and dinner alfresco draws to a close.

Contents

Introduction 8

CHAPTER ONE   **Early in the Morning** 13
Menu suggestions 14
Fruit dishes 16
Main dishes 20

CHAPTER TWO   **Drinks at Noon** 25
Menu suggestions 26
Non-alcoholic drinks 28

CHAPTER THREE   **Lunch Outdoors** 35
Menu suggestions 36
First courses 38
Salads and side dishes 42
Main dishes 46
Desserts 52

CHAPTER FOUR   **Afternoon Teas** 57
Menu suggestions 58
Sandwiches and breads 60
Cakes, tarts and cookies 64

CHAPTER FIVE   **Evening Drinks and Dips** 73
Menu suggestions 74
Alcoholic drinks 76
Nibbles and dips 82

CHAPTER SIX   **Barbecues** 89
Menu suggestions 90
Main dishes 92
Salads and side dishes 96
Desserts 104

CHAPTER SEVEN   **Light Suppers** 107
Menu suggestions 108
Main dishes 110
Salads and side dishes 116
Desserts 122

CHAPTER EIGHT   **Dinner at Dusk** 127
Menu suggestions 128
First courses 130
Main dishes 134
Salads and side dishes 138
Desserts 140

Index 144

INTRODUCTION

Eating out-of-doors in fine weather is one of summer's great pleasures. Meals eaten alfresco—in the open air—really do seem to taste better, whether they are spur-of-the-moment picnic breakfasts or elegant candlelit dinner parties. From spring through to autumn you can make memorable meals to eat outdoors—in the garden, on a roof terrace, in a meadow or wherever you choose.

The recipes in this book are grouped into chapters according to the time of day at which they can be served. Each chapter is divided into types of dish, such as salads, main dishes or desserts. Menu ideas at the beginning of each chapter suggest possible ways to combine the dishes.

However, many of the recipes are suitable for different courses and other times of day. Salads, for example, though usually served as accompaniments, can sometimes make perfect summertime main courses. Similarly, a fruit dish suggested for an informal breakfast alfresco could be equally suitable at the end of a formal dinner party.

There is no better time of year than summer for creating wonderful food. The choice of fabulous ingredients—tender soft fruits, aromatic herbs, crunchy vegetables—is virtually limitless.

Colourful fresh fruit epitomizes the beauty of summer and can be used in an infinite number of ways, from exotic fruit salads to icy sorbets.

The leaves of fresh herbs can be used to add flavour and fragrance to a great variety of dishes, while their flowers often make attractive garnishes. Borage, for example, is a beautiful and versatile herb. Its leaves, which taste rather like cucumber, are traditionally used in white wine punch and Pimm's No. 1 Cup, and its bright blue flowers can be widely used as a garnish.

The flavour of freshly picked local produce is unbeatable. It is said that corn on the cob should not even be picked until the cooking water is boiling!

SALAD GREENS

Of course, summer is *the* time for salads. These days there is a wide variety of salad leaves available.

Soft lettuces, known as butterhead (butter) or round lettuces, have a rich, slightly buttery flavour; Boston and Bibb are U.S. varieties, and All the Year Round is a British variety. The best known crisphead lettuces are iceberg and, in Britain, Webb's; these have a crunchy texture but less flavour than butterheads. Cos (romaine) has long, coarse, crisp leaves. Oak leaf, or leaf, lettuce is a type with no heart; it is useful for adding texture and colour to a salad. The variety of leaf lettuce known as Lollo Rosso (red leaf) has red-tinged frilly leaves.

Other greens also add flavour and variety to salads, including spinach, lamb's lettuce or mâche, and Chinese cabbage. Frisée or curly endive (often called curly chicory in the United States) has a distinctive bitter flavour and frilly leaves; its outer leaves are green and the inner ones pale. Chicory, or Belgian endive, is white and torpedo-shaped, with tightly closed leaves. Radicchio is a red-leaved variety of chicory, which has a similar slightly bitter flavour.

Many fresh herbs—including parsley, basil, chives, chervil, tarragon, fennel, marjoram, lovage, coriander, sweet rocket (arugula), sorrel and lemon balm—are delicious in salads.

EDIBLE FLOWERS

Also very good in salads are nasturtium leaves, which add an unusual, delicate flavour. They can be used in sauces and dressings, too, and the flowers make a beautiful, spicy-flavoured garnish for all manner of summer dishes. In fact, a large number of seasonal flowers are edible. Many others are not, however, so for safety's sake use only the following flowers: anchusa, sweet basil, red bergamot, borage, carnation, chamomile, chervil, chickweed, chive, chrysanthemum, clover, cornflower, courgette (zucchini), cowslip, daffodil, daisy, dandelion, dill, fennel, forget-me-not, grape hyacinth, hawthorn blossom, heartsease, hibiscus, hollyhock, honeysuckle, hop, hyssop, jasmine, lavender, lilac, day lily, tiger lily, lime (linden) blossom, lovage, magnolia, mallow, marjoram, pot marigold, mint, nasturtium, pansy, pink, poppy, primrose, rose, rosemary, sage, French sorrel, stocks, sweet Cicely, sweet woodruff, tansy, thyme, violet.

Edible flowers can be used whole, or the petals alone can be used. For roses, pinks, marigolds and cornflowers, pinch off the white "heel" from the base

of the petals, as it has a bitter taste. If you have bought the flowers from a florist, wash them in very cold water to remove any insecticides.

USING THE RECIPES

Because the recipes in this book make the most of seasonal ingredients, they are perfectly suited to summer meals alfresco: full of colour and flavour, yet light and wholesome. Part of the magic of alfresco dining is the element of spontaneity and freedom, so the dishes in this book are designed for simplicity and ease of preparation.

They derive from cultures all over the world— India, Indonesia, China, Mexico, France, Greece and Italy, as well as Britain and North America. All of the "foreign" ingredients are widely available here—if not from the local supermarket then from numerous delicatessens.

For example, **garam masala** is a mild blend of spices from India; it is widely available, both as a powder and as a paste. Or you could make your own, using three parts cardamom, three parts cinnamon, one part cloves and one part cumin. **Tahini** is an oily paste made from ground roasted sesame seeds, which is used in Middle Eastern cookery.

Greek yogurt is a thick, creamy yogurt made from whole milk and, often, extra cream. Most Greek yogurt is not live, nor is it low-fat—but it makes a delicious, less sweet alternative to cream as a topping for fruit dishes and desserts. If it is not available, however, thick plain yogurt could be substituted.

Fromage frais is a low-fat, very soft, moist cheese with a light texture and creamy taste. Made from pasteurized skimmed (skim) milk to a traditional French recipe, it is fermented for only a short time, hence the name (meaning "fresh cheese"). It is an excellent low-fat alternative to cream. If unavailable, soured (sour) cream may be substituted.

Crème fraîche is a lightly cultured cream with a consistency between soured (sour) cream and double (heavy) cream. If unavailable, you can substitute two parts double cream mixed with one part soured cream; leave in a warm room for 5–6 hours until thickened, then stir, cover and refrigerate. (However, if you are cooking with this substitute, stir it first over a low heat until it reaches 25°C/75°F. If you are using it with wine, treat it in the same way, but bring it up to boiling point. This treatment is not necessary for crème fraîche itself.)

Olive oil is used in many of the recipes in this book. If possible, use the highest-quality olive oil, known as extra virgin, which comes from the first cold pressing of the olives. Also occasionally featuring in the recipes are **walnut oil**, made from walnuts, and **sesame oil**, from sesame seeds; both have a nutty flavour and are delicious in salads, particularly those made from the more bitter salad leaves such as radicchio and endive.

SETTING THE SCENE

Alfresco meals can be as elegant or informal as the occasion demands. Wherever you are eating, you can set the scene with your choice of table setting. It's amazing what a pretty tablecloth, vase of summer flowers and cheerful napkins, plates, cutlery and glasses can do! Hidden beneath them might be a couple of folding card tables, an old wallpapering table, or even a door resting on two crates. If necessary, anchor the tablecloth securely with clips, tape or weights. The table should be set up in a shady spot not too far from the kitchen, along with chairs, travelling rugs (picnic blankets) and cushions for people to sit on.

In the evening, hurricane lamps and candles create a terrific atmosphere. Candles can be protected from the wind inside glass jars or in candle lanterns or set into sand inside large brown paper bags.

If you are entertaining a group of people, be sure to provide more plates, glasses, cutlery and napkins than the number of guests. You can use cool bags and boxes, as well as thermos flasks, to keep food hot or cold and reduce the number of trips to the kitchen.

PICNICS

Insulated carriers are useful for alfresco meals in the garden, but they have revolutionized picnics. Food that is transported in them, or in any other carrier, should be covered securely with aluminium foil or cling film (plastic wrap), double-wrapped for safety. Cheese and cooked meats can be packed in polythene (plastic) bags, and delicate foods in rigid airtight containers. To pack foods that you want to keep chilled, wrap them in newspaper along with pre-frozen freezer blocks before putting in the cool box or bag. Hot foods can be kept hot in these insulated carriers too, but not for as long a time.

Transport cold drinks and soups in narrow-necked thermos flasks, and solid foods in wide-necked flasks. Preparing the flasks in advance helps: for cold drinks chill the flask before filling it, and for hot drinks rinse the flask first with boiling water. If possible, fill it to the top to keep the contents cold/hot for a longer time. Take milk for tea in a separate sealed carton or tightly closed screw-top jar covered with cling film (plastic wrap). Salad dressing should be packed in the same way.

The best food for picnics is food that tastes good cold, is not too heavy to carry or too fragile to survive the journey, and can be eaten easily with the fingers or a minimum of cutlery. Salads travel well, packed in airtight containers, with the dressing added just prior to serving. Sponge cakes wrapped in cling film (plastic wrap) and, of course, fresh fruit are also ideal for picnics—as are many of the recipes in this book. Where applicable, special instructions for picnics are given with the recipes.

Old-fashioned wicker picnic hampers are very luxurious and are a convenient way to transport cups, glasses, plates and cutlery. But they may prove impractical if you need a lot of space for food or for all those essential extras like a corkscrew, can opener, bread knife, paper towels, and packets of salt and pepper. A capacious wicker basket with a handle, lined with a gingham cloth, is an equally stylish alternative to the traditional hamper.

Don't forget to take along picnic chairs and travelling rugs (picnic blankets) if required. You might even want to consider a small portable barbecue.

Picnics—in fact, all outdoor meals—can be as elaborate or simple as you make them. On one occasion, you and your friends or family may decide to indulge in an open-air feast with all the trimmings. Another time you may choose just to pack a simple snack, some fruit and a bottle of Chablis and head for the hills. That is the beauty of eating alfresco.

CHAPTER ONE

Early in the Morning

The beauty and freshness of early summer mornings are the rewards for planning an alfresco breakfast, whether it is a simple picnic in the countryside or a full-scale meal on the patio. Colourful summer fruits provide a glorious start to the day, and are an excellent prelude to an egg or fish course. Take your picnic to a meadow or riverbank, or just out into the garden, and enjoy breakfast alfresco before the rest of the world awakens!

MENU SUGGESTIONS

MENU 1
Golden Grapefruit Brûlée page 16
Hot Waffles with Strawberry Sauce page 20

•

MENU 2
Fresh Fruit Salad page 16
Scrambled Eggs with Smoked Eel page 20

•

MENU 3
Frozen Berry Yogurt page 19
Buckwheat Kedgeree page 21

•

MENU 4
Berries with Dried Fruit page 16
Eggs in Pitta Pockets page 22

•

MENU 5
Sunshine Fruit Bowl page 19
Grilled (Broiled) Tomatoes on Fried Bread page 23

•

MENU 6
Summer Fruit Bowl page 19
Mushroom Toasts with Marjoram page 22

FRUIT DISHES

BERRIES WITH DRIED FRUIT

This summer breakfast looks as lovely as it tastes: there is a Mexican saying that food must pass through the eyes before it enters the mouth! In both respects this is a beautiful way to start the day. You can garnish it with geranium petals or clover flowers.

SERVES 6–8

225 g (8 oz/1⅓ cups) dried fruits, such as apricots, prunes, figs, raisins
600 ml (1 pint/2½ cups) orange juice
grated rind of 1 lemon
1 banana
225 g (8 oz/1½ cups) strawberries or raspberries, stalks and hulls removed
Greek yogurt (see page 9), to serve

1 Soak the dried fruits in the orange juice with the grated lemon rind overnight.
2 In the morning, peel the banana and slice it into the compote. Cut the strawberries in half if using. Fold the strawberries or raspberries in also.
3 Serve each helping topped with thick Greek yogurt.

GOLDEN GRAPEFRUIT BRÛLÉE

This refreshing breakfast dish is served with the topping hot, and just beginning to crystallize and harden; the grapefruit beneath remains alluringly cool. A perfect start to a summer's day.

SERVES 4

2 large ripe grapefruit, halved
60 ml (4 tbsp) dark orange marmalade
60 ml (4 tbsp) demerara (light brown) sugar

1 Loosen the grapefruit segments with a serrated knife. Spread 15 ml (1 tbsp) marmalade over the top of each half and sprinkle with 15 ml (1 tbsp) sugar.
2 Place under a hot grill (broiler) for 1–2 minutes until the sugar melts and the marmalade bubbles. Leave for a minute or so to cool a little before serving.

FRESH FRUIT SALAD

The fruits of the summer season, with their fresh taste and lovely colours, epitomize the joy of eating alfresco. Fresh fruit salad makes a scrumptious alfresco breakfast, particularly on a picnic. Decorate the fruit with a few flowers, such as bergamot, cornflower, hawthorn or mallow—whatever is growing nearby.

SELECT FROM:
bananas, peeled and sliced
pears, peeled and chopped
seedless grapes, halved and peeled if desired
crisp apples, thinly sliced
satsumas (tangerines), peeled and segmented
passion fruit, halved then flesh scooped out and sieved
kiwi fruit, peeled and sliced
black cherries, stoned (pitted), stalked and halved
guavas, peeled and chopped
mangoes, peeled, stoned (pitted) and chopped
pineapple, cored and finely sliced
preserved ginger, chopped
nectarines or peaches, skinned, stoned (pitted) and sliced
fresh figs, quartered
wild strawberries, hulled
golden or purple plums, stoned (pitted) and sliced

1 Prepare the chosen fruits and put them into a large glass bowl or container for transporting.
2 To every 450 g (1 lb) fruit add 300 ml (½ pint/1¼ cups) orange juice or tropical fruit juice. Chill.

RIGHT: *Melon with Berries (page 19)*

FRUIT WITH YOGURT

Fruit with Greek yogurt (see page 9) is delightful as a light breakfast to eat in the early morning sunshine. There is no limit to the dazzling colour combinations you can create using a variety of fruits. Here are four simple but dramatic ideas.

FROZEN BERRY YOGURT

1 Fold frozen bilberries or blueberries into Greek yogurt.
2 Dribble clear honey over, then chill. Serve very cold for a refreshing summer breakfast. Garnish the dish with berries or a sprig of blue anchusa if available.

SUMMER FRUIT BOWL

1 Combine black grapes, blueberries, wedges of fig and sliced plums in a bowl. Decorate with pomegranate seeds.
2 If desired, dip the fruits into caster (superfine) sugar. Top with thick Greek yogurt before eating.

SUNSHINE FRUIT BOWL

1 Combine bananas, kiwi fruit, green apples, sliced kumquats, sliced star fruit (carambola) and green grapes in a bowl.
2 To every 450 g (1 lb/1 quart) of fruit add 300 ml ($\frac{1}{2}$ pint/$1\frac{1}{4}$ cups) orange juice or tropical fruit juice. Chill. Serve with Greek yogurt.

MELON WITH BERRIES

1 Cut a melon in half and remove the seeds.
2 Fill the hollow with blueberries, and garnish with a strawberry. Serve with Greek yogurt.
Illustrated on page 17

Full many a glorious morning have I seen
Flatter the mountain-tops with sovereign eye,
Kissing with golden face the meadows green,
Gilding pale streams with heavenly alchemy;
William Shakespeare: "Sonnets"

LEFT *(clockwise from top):* Frozen Berry Yogurt *(page 19),* Sunshine Fruit Bowl *(page 19),* Summer Fruit Bowl *(page 19)*

MAIN DISHES

HOT WAFFLES WITH STRAWBERRY SAUCE

Freshly made waffles make a mouthwatering breakfast—the aroma is irresistible. You can serve them with butter and/or maple syrup, but for a beautiful summer's day this Strawberry Sauce is unbeatable. You can prepare the batter the night before and leave it to stand in a cool place (not the refrigerator) covered with cling film (plastic wrap).

MAKES 6

225 g (8 oz/2 cups) plain (all-purpose) flour
15 ml (1 tbsp) baking powder
2.5 ml ($\frac{1}{2}$ tsp) salt
15 ml (1 tbsp) caster (superfine) sugar
2 eggs, separated
350 ml (12 fl oz/1$\frac{1}{2}$ cups) milk
75 g (3 oz/6 tbsp) margarine, melted
FOR THE STRAWBERRY SAUCE
450 g (1 lb/3 cups) strawberries, stalks and hulls
removed
caster (superfine) sugar, to taste

1 Sift the flour with the baking powder, salt and sugar into a bowl. Beat the egg yolks with the milk, but do

not overbeat or the waffles will be hard. Stir in the melted margarine, then stir into the dry ingredients.
2 Just before making the waffles, beat the egg whites to stiff peaks and fold into the batter. Cook the waffles according to the directions on your waffle iron. Place on a wire rack, rather than stacking them on a plate, and keep warm in a cool oven.
3 To make the sauce, purée the strawberries and sugar in a food processor or blender until liquid. Pass through a sieve to separate out the seeds. Chill. Spoon the sauce over the hot waffles as you eat them.

SCRAMBLED EGGS WITH SMOKED EEL

Although smoked eel is not widely available, it can often be found, filleted or on the bone, at delicatessens. The puff pastry triangles can be made the night before if preferred.

PER PERSON

2 puff pastry triangles (see method)
beaten egg, for glazing
2 eggs
30 ml (2 tbsp) milk
salt and pepper
50 g (2 oz/$\frac{1}{4}$ cup) smoked eel, diced small
15 g ($\frac{1}{2}$ oz/1 tbsp) butter or margarine

1 To make the puff pastry triangles, roll out puff pastry to about 3 mm ($\frac{1}{8}$ inch) on a floured work surface. Cut into triangles with about 10 cm (4 inch) sides. Place on a baking sheet and brush with beaten egg. Bake at 220°C/425°F/mark 7 for 6–8 minutes until risen and golden. If making the night before, reheat in the morning at 170°C/325°F/mark 3 for 6–8 minutes.
2 For the scrambled eggs, beat the eggs thoroughly with the milk and add salt and pepper. Fold in the diced smoked eel. Heat the butter in a saucepan and scramble lightly until set but still moist and creamy.
3 Serve the eel mixture in the centre of a warm plate, with the golden pastry triangles on either side.

BUCKWHEAT KEDGEREE

Kedgeree, a classic English breakfast dish, makes a wonderful meal alfresco, and this is a kedgeree with a difference. The smoky aroma of both the haddock and the buckwheat are sensational. Serve it to guests for a late, lingering weekend breakfast on the patio, with lots of tea and coffee. A bread basket full of croissants, decorated with a sprig of wild flowers, serves as the perfect centrepiece.

SERVES 4

225 g (8 oz) smoked haddock
15 ml (1 tbsp) sunflower oil
100 g (4 oz/scant $\frac{1}{2}$ cup) buckwheat
250 ml (8 fl oz/1 cup) water
2 hard-boiled eggs
25 g (1 oz/2 tbsp) butter

salt and pepper
pinch of cayenne pepper
chopped fresh parsley, to garnish

1 Cover the haddock with boiling water and leave to stand for 5 minutes. Remove any bones and skin, then flake the flesh.
2 Heat the oil in a pan and stir in the buckwheat over a medium heat until it begins to "pop". After the "popping" has diminished, pour the water over and bring to simmering point. Simmer gently for 15 minutes or until tender, stirring occasionally.
3 Meanwhile chop the whites of the eggs and sieve the yolks.
4 Stir the flaked fish, egg whites and butter into the cooked buckwheat. Add lots of salt and pepper, and a pinch of cayenne.
5 Pile the kedgeree on to a warm dish and garnish with the sieved egg yolk. Scatter chopped parsley over the top and serve.

MUSHROOM TOASTS WITH MARJORAM

The fragrance of fresh marjoram spells summer, sunshine, shimmering heat. This herb has a special affinity with mushrooms—a fact recognized by the Italians, who combine the two ingredients in this delicious way. It was in Italy that I first breakfasted on this dish, among the rolling hills and cypress trees of Umbria, the "green heart" of the country.

SERVES 4

6 very large flat mushrooms, wiped
30 ml (2 tbsp) chopped fresh marjoram
olive oil
8 slices of bread
salt and pepper

1 Slice the mushrooms about 5 mm ($\frac{1}{4}$ inch) thick. Put them in a bowl with the marjoram, then pour olive oil over them and toss until well coated with both.
2 Heat a metal baking sheet under a hot grill (broiler) and, when really hot, pour in enough olive oil to coat the surface. As soon as the oil is hot, place the mushrooms in the tray and grill (broil), turning occasionally, until cooked through. Put into a warm oven while preparing the bread.
3 Brush the slices of bread generously with olive oil and brown them under the grill. Place the mushrooms on the prepared toast, add salt and pepper to taste and serve immediately.

The glory of the beauty of the morning—
The cuckoo crying over the untouched dew;
The blackbird that has found it, and the dove
That tempts me on to something sweeter than love;
White clouds ranged even and fair as new-mown hay;
The heat, the stir, the sublime vacancy
Of sky and meadow and forest and my own heart:—
Edward Thomas: "The Glory"

EGGS IN PITTA POCKETS

Pitta bread is a flat, hollow, unleavened bread from the Middle East which can be slit in half lengthwise to reveal the "pocket" inside. Pitta pockets are traditionally filled with shredded lettuce, onion rings, and cucumber and tomato slices, but a filling of fried egg is an unusual and surprisingly delicious alternative. The firm texture of pitta bread makes them ideal for a picnic breakfast or brunch. They work very well if you make them the night before, wrap them in cling film (plastic wrap) and keep them refrigerated until you set off.

SERVES 4

60 ml (4 tbsp) vegetable oil, for frying
4 eggs
salt and pepper
4 pitta breads
butter or spreadable margarine

1 Heat the oil in a heavy frying pan until very hot. Fry the eggs quickly until the whites are browned and crisp, but the yolk is still slightly runny. Lift out carefully and drain on paper towels. Add salt and pepper, then cool completely.
2 Slit open the pitta breads and spread the insides lightly with butter or margarine. Slip one egg inside each and press down gently.
3 Serve these at once, or wrap them in cling film (plastic wrap) to take on a picnic.

GRILLED (BROILED) TOMATOES ON FRIED BREAD

This always reminds me of holiday breakfasts on a Greek beach, with the sun shining relentlessly on to white sand and a calm azure sea. We would sit under beach umbrellas and eat this simple feast with strong Greek coffee. The tomatoes were sun-ripened, of course, and at the height of their season.

SERVES 4

2 very large tomatoes
salt and pepper
dried oregano

ABOVE: Grilled (Broiled) Tomatoes on Fried Bread (this page)

30 ml (2 tbsp) olive oil
8 slices of bread, crusts removed

1 Slice the tomatoes thinly crosswise. Place on a grill (broiler) pan and sprinkle with salt and pepper and dried oregano. Dribble olive oil over them.
2 Grill (broil) for about 2 minutes until the tomatoes begin to soften, then grill on the other side. Keep warm.
3 Cut the bread in half, and fry in more olive oil, turning so that both sides are evenly golden and crisp. Drain on paper towels.
4 Place the tomato slices on top of the fried bread, and serve immediately.

CHAPTER TWO

Drinks at Noon

At the height of summer, long, cold drinks at midday make a refreshing break. Summer fruits provide cooling cordials, decorated with flower blossoms or sprigs of herbs which capture the fragrances of midsummer. Relax in a shady spot in the garden with tall glasses of Lemon Balm Cup or Rose Cordial, or take along a thermos flask of Minted Grape Juice or Tropical Fruit Cup on a stroll in the countryside. A delightful way to enjoy the fruits of the season.

LEFT: Tropical Fruit Cup (page 28)

MENU SUGGESTIONS

MENU 7
Lemon Balm Cup page 32
Rose Cordial page 31
Smoked Salmon Rolls page 130
Miniature Chicken Patties page 48

•

MENU 8
Tropical Fruit Cup page 28
Minted Grape Juice page 31
Filo Party Pieces page 82

•

MENU 9
Mangoade page 32
Exotic Refresco page 32
Tzatziki with Dill page 38, *served with strips of pitta bread*

•

MENU 10
Chilled Mint Tea page 28
Focaccia alla Caprese page 48, *cut into slivers*

•

MENU 11
Blueberry Lassi page 28
Oriental Pâté page 38, *served with crudités*

NON-ALCOHOLIC DRINKS

BLUEBERRY LASSI

Lassi is a cooling yogurt drink served in India and the tropics. Flavoured with blueberries, it not only tastes wonderful but also has the most beautiful and unique colour. An unforgettable midday refreshment while sitting on the patio.

MAKES 600 ml (1 pint/2½ cups)

225 g (8 oz/2 cups) blueberries
225 g (8 oz/1 cup) plain yogurt
90 ml (6 tbsp) caster (superfine) sugar
ice cubes

1 Purée the blueberries, yogurt and sugar in a blender or food processor. Pass through a sieve to separate the liquid from the skins. Chill.
2 To serve, put a couple of ice cubes into a tall glass and pour the Lassi over them.

TROPICAL FRUIT CUP

This fruit cup is wonderful for a group of people on a summer's day. It looks lovely with fresh fruit floating on top, decorated with mint and basil leaves and the colourful flowers of borage.

SERVES 8–10

600 ml (1 pint/2½ cups) orange juice, chilled
2.3 litres (4 pints/10 cups) grape juice, chilled
1 litre (1¾ pints/4¼ cups) tropical fruit juice, chilled
1.7 litres (3 pints/7½ cups) sparkling mineral water, chilled
prepared fresh fruit, such as kiwi fruit, strawberry, lemon slices, raspberries, grapes
ice cubes
TO DECORATE
mint leaves
basil leaves
borage flowers (optional)

1 Mix all the chilled liquids in a large bowl just before serving. Float the prepared fruit on top.
2 Scatter the mint and basil leaves over the fruit, then drop in the little borage flowers if available.
3 Ladle the drink into large wine glasses, with an ice cube or two in each one.

CHILLED MINT TEA

A small patch of mint grows near my garden gate, and I allow it to spread where it wants. It makes wonderful tea: this chilled mint tea is one of the most refreshing drinks for hot summer days.

SERVES 2–3

600 ml (1 pint/2½ cups) boiling water
4 large mint sprigs
caster (superfine) sugar, for frosting glasses

1 Pour the boiling water over the mint in a medium teapot. Cover and allow to infuse for 10 minutes. Strain and cool, then chill.
2 For frosted glasses, dip the rims of tall glasses into 5 mm (¼ inch) water, shake and dip into caster (superfine) sugar.
3 Serve the tea in the frosted glasses.

Lo, the most excellent sun so calm and haughty,
The violet and purple morn with just-felt breezes,
The gentle soft-born measureless light,
The miracle spreading bathing all, the fulfill'd noon,
The coming eve delicious, the welcome night and the stars,
Over my cities shining all, enveloping man and land.
Walt Whitman: "When Lilacs Last in the Dooryard Bloom'd"

RIGHT: *Tropical Fruit Cup (this page)*

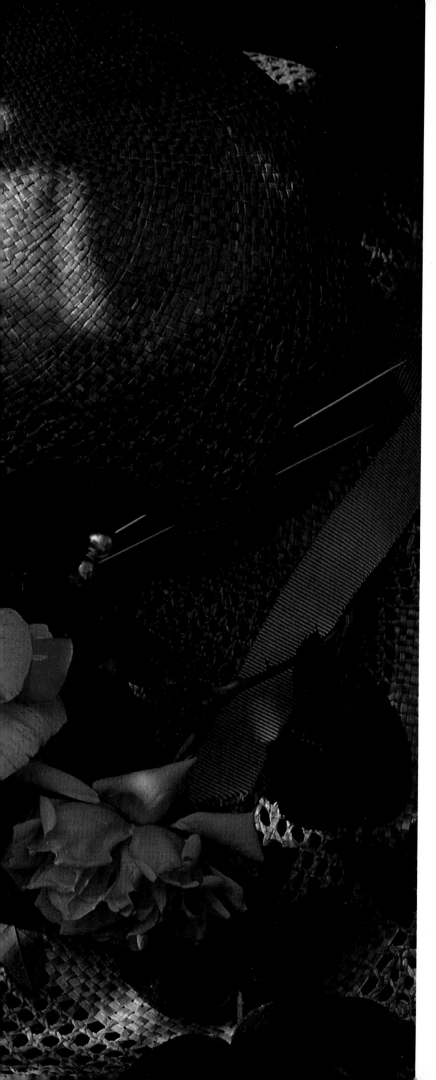

ROSE CORDIAL

Midsummer fragrances are captured in this lovely cordial. Pink rose petals floated on the top make it an elegant drink to serve in the garden to friends in high summer. If possible, use petals from wild roses.

MAKES 2.3 litres (4 pints/2½ quarts)

20 heads of scented rose petals, plus extra petals to decorate
900 g (2 lb/4 cups) granulated sugar
2.3 litres (4 pints/2½ quarts) boiled water, cold
½ lemon, sliced
sparkling mineral water

1 Remove the rose petals from the heads. Put them into a large pan with the sugar, water and lemon slices. Stir periodically for 24 hours. Strain and bottle.
2 Dilute to taste with the water. Float the rose petals on the top, removing the white "heels" first.

MINTED GRAPE JUICE

Here lemon and mint are marinated in grape juice to make a cooling long drink. If you have heartsease in the garden, sprinkle some petals among the diced pears and seedless grape halves.

SERVES 4

2 lemons, sliced
6 mint sprigs
1.1 litres (2 pints/5 cups) grape juice
icing (confectioners') sugar, to taste
100 g (4 oz/1 cup) seedless grapes, halved
1 ripe pear or kiwifruit, skinned and diced
heartsease petals (optional)

1 Place the lemon slices and mint in a bowl and marinate in the grape juice for a few hours or overnight.
2 Sweeten to taste with the sugar, then pour into a large jug (pitcher). Float the grapes and diced pear on top of the juice. Chill thoroughly.
3 Just before serving, sprinkle the juice with the flower petals, if available.

LEMON BALM CUP

The refreshing combination of lemon with apple makes a cooling midday drink in spring and early summer. The sprigs of lemon balm—a herb that is perfect for fruit juices and wine cups, adding sweetness and a lemony flavour—give off their delicate scent as you sip the drink, evoking fine days of sunshine and the first herbs of the season.

SERVES 4

600 ml (1 pint/2½ cups) fizzy lemonade (lemon soda), chilled
600 ml (1 pint/2½ cups) apple juice, chilled
4 slices of lemon
¼ crisp red apple, thinly sliced
ice cubes
8 lemon balm sprigs

1 Mix the lemonade (lemon soda) and apple juice with the sliced fruit in a large jug (pitcher). Add the ice, and float sprigs of lemon balm on the top.
2 Pour the drink into tall glasses to serve, with a sprig of lemon balm in each one.

MANGOADE

This fruit drink is sublime: the inimitable delicacy of mangoes is balanced by fresh orange juice, and the texture is wonderful. Soft and sweet, it is perfect for a summer's day sitting in the garden, or basking in the warmth of a conservatory or sunporch.

SERVES 4–6

450 g (1 lb/2 cups) ripe mango flesh, coarsely chopped
50 g (2 oz/¼ cup) granulated sugar or to taste
450 ml (¾ pint/2 cups) sparkling mineral water
5 ml (1 tsp) grated orange rind
450 ml (¾ pint/2 cups) orange juice
ice cubes
TO DECORATE
slices of lime
rose petals (optional)

1 Purée the mango in a blender or food processor.

2 Combine the sugar, water and orange rind in a saucepan and heat, stirring, until the sugar dissolves. Cool, then add to the mango with the juice. Chill.
3 Serve on ice, in tall glasses, decorated with a slice of lime. Add a few rose petals if available, removing the white "heels" first.

EXOTIC REFRESCO

Exotic indeed, this special-occasion recipe is based on a Caribbean idea and looks sensational decorated with a few hibiscus flowers.

SERVES 3–4

25 g (1 oz/¼ cup) creamed coconut or 40 g (1½ oz/⅜ cup) desiccated (shredded dried) coconut
175 ml (6 fl oz/¾ cup) boiling water
1 ripe papaya or mango, peeled
45 ml (3 tbsp) lime juice
2.5 ml (½ tsp) grated lime rind
50 g (2 oz/¼ cup) caster (superfine) sugar
5 ml (1 tsp) vanilla extract
caster (superfine) sugar, for frosting glasses
finely crushed ice
TO DECORATE
hibiscus flowers (optional)
slices of lime

1 To make the coconut milk, cut the creamed coconut into small pieces and dissolve in the boiling water. Alternatively, steep the desiccated (shredded dried) coconut in the boiling water for 1 hour, and strain through muslin (cheesecloth), discarding the pulp.
2 Cut the papaya or mango in half, remove the seeds or stone (pit) and chop the flesh coarsely. Purée the papaya or mango flesh, coconut milk, lime juice and rind, sugar and vanilla in a blender or food processor until smooth and thick.
3 For frosted glasses, dip the rims of glasses into 5 mm (¼ inch) water, shake and dip into caster (superfine) sugar. Chill the glasses.
4 Serve the purée on crushed ice, in the chilled frosted glasses. Float hibiscus flowers, if available, and slices of lime on the top.

RIGHT: *Lemon Balm Cup (this page)*

CHAPTER THREE

Lunch Outdoors

A cold menu is tailormade for summertime lunches alfresco. Not only is such a meal the most appealing on a hot day, but it can be prepared in advance so that you have more time to relax with family or guests. Cold dishes are also ideal for picnics. Whether you are lunching in your own garden or on the beach, in a roof terrace or by a mountain stream, lay out the food on a pretty tablecloth, and enjoy the beauty of a meal in the sunshine.

MENU SUGGESTIONS

MENU 12
Chilled Cucumber Soup page 40
Creamy Ginger Chicken page 51
Mangetout (Snow Pea) and New Potato Salad page 44
Pasta Salad with Basil and Cheese page 45
Black Currant Shortcake page 122

•

MENU 13
Tzatziki with Dill page 38, *served with pitta bread strips and
raw cauliflower florets*
Picnic Omelette Fines Herbes page 49
Focaccia alla Caprese page 48
Green Salad with Walnut Oil Dressing page 42

•

MENU 14
Oriental Pâté page 38, *served with toast*
Tagliatelle with Fennel page 46
Chicory (Endive) and Celery Salad page 44
Blackberry Sorbet page 54

•

MENU 15
Provençal Stuffed Tomatoes page 44
Chunky Chicken Patties page 48
Pepper and Rice Salad page 42
Light Mint Ice Cream page 52

•

MENU 16
Chervil Soufflé-omelette page 46
Mussels and Pasta Twists with Basil page 49
tossed green salad
Individual Summer Puddings page 52

FIRST COURSES

ORIENTAL PÂTÉ

You can eat this aubergine (eggplant) purée as a pâté or as a dip—so serve it either with toast and a little side salad, or with strips of pitta bread and a selection of crudités. Gently spiced, soft and smooth, it is ideal for warm weather.

SERVES 4

2 medium aubergines (eggplants)
4 small garlic cloves, skinned and sliced
10 ml (2 tsp) grated fresh ginger root
sea salt
15 ml (1 tbsp) chopped spring onion (scallion)
15 ml (1 tbsp) chopped fresh coriander
2.5 ml ($\frac{1}{2}$ tsp) garam masala (see page 9)

1 Cut slits in the aubergine (eggplant) skin and insert the garlic slices into them. Bake at 180°C/350°F/mark 4 for 25 minutes until completely soft. Cool.
2 Skin the aubergine, removing the garlic. Mash the pulp with the grated ginger and add sea salt to taste.
3 Fold in the onion, coriander and garam masala, blending until smooth. Chill.

Smile O voluptuous cool-breath'd earth!
Earth of the slumbering and liquid trees!
Earth of departed sunset—earth of the
mountains misty-topt!
Earth of the vitreous pour of the full moon
just tinged with blue!
Earth of shine and dark mottling the tide of the river!
Earth of the limpid gray of clouds brighter and
clearer for my sake!
Far-swooping elbow'd earth—rich apple-blossom'd earth!
Smile, for your lover comes.
Walt Whitman: "Song of Myself"

TZATZIKI WITH DILL

A summer standby, Tzatziki is a Mediterranean dip with many variations. This one, with dill rather than garlic, has a particularly delicate flavour and is delicious served with strips of pitta bread and slices of raw cauliflower. If you have stocks growing in the garden, garnish the dip with a few of the flowers—pale pink or white ones look good around the edge of this pale green dish.

SERVES 4

$\frac{1}{2}$ medium cucumber, peeled
30 ml (2 tbsp) chopped fresh dill
350 g (12 oz/1$\frac{1}{2}$ cups) plain yogurt
sea salt, to taste
stock flowers, to garnish (optional)

1 Grate the cucumber coarsely, then pat it dry on paper towels.
2 Mix the chopped dill into the yogurt. Add a little sea salt to taste. Fold in the grated cucumber and mix thoroughly.
3 Put the dip into a bowl and cover with cling film (plastic wrap). Chill thoroughly before serving. Garnish with stocks if available.

CHILLED CUCUMBER SOUP

This fresh, cooling soup is just right for a picnic, or it could be served for lunch in the garden. Its delicate pale-green colour is accented by borage flowers.

SERVES 4

1 large cucumber, peeled
10 ml (2 tsp) lemon rind
30 ml (2 tbsp) lemon juice
1 garlic clove, skinned and crushed
450 g (1 lb/2 cups) plain yogurt
30 ml (2 tbsp) chopped chives
15 ml (1 tbsp) chopped fresh parsley
salt and pepper
paprika
borage flowers, to garnish (optional)

1 Cut 12 thin slices off the cucumber and reserve for garnish.
2 Chop the rest of the cucumber and put into a blender or food processor with the lemon rind and juice, garlic, yogurt, chives and parsley. Blend until smooth. Add salt, pepper and paprika to taste. Chill.
3 Serve very cold, garnished with the reserved cucumber slices and borage flowers if available.

We know the dog-rose, flinging free
Whip-lashes in the hedgerow, starred with pale
Shell blossom as a Canterbury Tale,
The candid English genius, fresh and pink
As Chaucer made us think,
Singing of adolescent meads in May.
That's not the rose in her true character;
She's a voluptuary; think of her
Wine-dark and heavy-scented of the South,
Stuck in a cap or dangled from a mouth
As soft as her own petals. That's the rose!
Vita Sackville-West: "The Garden"

RIGHT: *Chilled Cucumber Soup (this page)*

SALADS & SIDE DISHES

GREEN SALAD WITH WALNUT OIL DRESSING

A simple salad of mixed lettuce leaves and chopped chives makes a superb end to an alfresco meal, be it a picnic or an elegant dinner party. The distinctive heavy taste of walnut oil is balanced by the fresh sharpness of lemon juice in this summery dressing.

SERVES 6

2 soft lettuces, trimmed
2 small cos (romaine) lettuces, trimmed
1 leaf lettuce, trimmed
medium-sized bunch of chives, finely chopped
FOR THE WALNUT OIL DRESSING
60 ml (4 tbsp) walnut oil (see page 10)
juice of 1 lemon
5 ml (1 tsp) soy sauce
salt and pepper

1 To make the Walnut Oil Dressing, combine the oil, lemon juice and soy sauce in a screw-top jar, and shake vigorously until well blended. Add salt and pepper to taste.
2 Mix the greens in a large salad bowl with the chives. Toss with the dressing just before serving.

PEPPER AND RICE SALAD

A salad of peppers, grilled (broiled) so that they turn slightly sweet, and combined with rice and herbs, makes a delightful summery dish. Garnish with tomato wedges around the edge and, if possible, a few cornflowers scattered over the top.

SERVES 4

pinch of garam masala (see page 9)
75 ml (5 tbsp) Vinaigrette (see this page)
175 g (6 oz/scant 1 cup) long grain rice
1 red pepper, quartered
1 yellow pepper, quartered
30 ml (2 tbsp) finely chopped fresh mixed herbs, such as tarragon, fennel, marjoram, chives or lovage
TO GARNISH
tomato wedges
cornflowers (optional)

1 Add a pinch of garam masala to the Vinaigrette and leave to stand.
2 Cook the rice in a saucepan of boiling salted water until tender. Cool the cooked rice immediately under running cold water.
3 Grill (broil) the peppers, skin side up, for 5–10 minutes or until the skins blister. Cool, then peel and remove seeds. Cut the flesh into tiny shreds.
4 Mix the rice, peppers and herbs together. Dress in the spiced Vinaigrette. Put into a shallow serving dish. Surround with the wedges of tomato and scatter with some cornflowers if available, removing the white "heels" first. Serve at room temperature.

VINAIGRETTE

Vinaigrette is the most widely used salad dressing. This version is made from oil and vinegar in a ratio of 5:1, which is particularly well suited to delicately flavoured lettuces. For salads incorporating more strongly flavoured greens, beans or root vegetables, you may prefer to make the oil/vinegar ratio 4:1. The flavour of the dressing will depend to a large extent on the quality of oil you use. Good-quality (extra virgin) olive oil gives it a fruity flavour which is less bland than sunflower oil.

MAKES 190 ml ($6\frac{1}{2}$ fl oz/$\frac{3}{4}$ cup)

150 ml ($\frac{1}{4}$ pint/$\frac{2}{3}$ cup) olive oil
10 ml (2 tsp) Dijon mustard
30 ml (2 tbsp) tarragon vinegar
salt and pepper

1 Combine all the ingredients in a screw-top jar.
2 Shake vigorously until well blended.

CHICORY (ENDIVE) AND CELERY SALAD

The delicate pale greens of this salad make a striking contrast with slices of orange. Lime (linden) flowers look beautiful as garnish.

SERVES 4

8 celery sticks, trimmed and sliced crosswise
2 large heads of chicory (endive), diagonally sliced
1 fennel bulb, very finely sliced
2 oranges, peeled
40 g (1½ oz/scant ½ cup) walnuts, chopped
lime (linden) blossom, to garnish (optional)
FOR THE ORANGE-AND-GINGER DRESSING
30 ml (2 tbsp) orange juice
2.5 cm (1 inch) piece fresh ginger root, peeled and finely grated
20 ml (4 tsp) Vinaigrette (see page 42)
20 ml (4 tsp) plain yogurt

1 To make the Orange-and-ginger Dressing, combine the ingredients in a screw-top jar and shake vigorously. Leave to stand for at least 30 minutes.
2 Combine the celery, chicory (endive) and fennel in a salad bowl. Cut the peeled orange in half, remove all the seeds and pith, and slice the flesh finely. Add to the salad ingredients with the walnuts and mix in.
3 Just before serving, add the dressing. Garnish with lime (linden) blossom if available.

MANGETOUT (SNOW PEA) AND NEW POTATO SALAD

In this pretty salad, the delicate ivory colour of new potatoes is combined with the fresh green of mangetout (snow peas). It looks stunning surrounded by watercress and with one or two hibiscus flowers on top.

SERVES 4

450 g (1 lb) small new potatoes, scrubbed
175 g (6 oz) mangetout (snow peas), trimmed
2 bunches of watercress
hibiscus flowers, to garnish (optional)
FOR THE RASPBERRY VINEGAR MAYONNAISE
15 ml (1 tbsp) raspberry vinegar
5 ml (1 tsp) soy sauce
45 ml (3 tbsp) Homemade Mayonnaise (see page 101)

1 To make the Raspberry Vinegar Mayonnaise, stir the raspberry vinegar and soy sauce into the mayonnaise. Mix thoroughly.
2 Cook the new potatoes in their skins in a saucepan of boiling salted water until waxy and still slightly crisp. Plunge them into cold water immediately to cool.
3 Steam the mangetout (snow peas) for 2 minutes, so that they also remain slightly crisp. Slice them diagonally into 5 mm (¼ inch) wide strips.
4 Quarter the potatoes and mix with the mangetout. Toss in the Raspberry Vinegar Mayonnaise.
5 Put the salad into a serving dish and surround with the watercress. If possible, scatter one or two hibiscus flowers on top just before eating.

PROVENÇAL STUFFED TOMATOES

An ideal dish for a summer buffet table set in a shady spot in the garden. Place the stuffed tomatoes on a bed of lettuce leaves on a platter, and garnish them with sprigs of parsley and black olives.

SERVES 4

4 very large tomatoes
2 garlic cloves, skinned and crushed
15 ml (1 tbsp) chopped fresh parsley
100 g (4 oz/1 cup) medium-hard goat's cheese, grated
15 ml (1 tbsp) wholegrain mustard such as Moutarde de Meaux
50 g (2 oz/¼ cup) cooked rice
225 g (8 oz/1 cup) fromage frais (see page 9)
sea salt and pepper
TO GARNISH
black olives
parsley sprigs

1 Cut the top off each tomato and reserve the lids. Scoop out the central flesh.
2 Purée the flesh with the garlic in a blender or food

processor until smooth. Add the parsley, cheese and mustard, then stir in the rice and fromage frais. Add sea salt and pepper to taste.

3 Pack the cheese mixture into the tomato shells and replace the lids. Chill. Garnish the stuffed tomatoes with olives and sprigs of parsley.

PASTA SALAD WITH BASIL AND CHEESE

This summer vegetable and pasta salad is aromatic with herbs and the inimitable smell of fresh Parmesan. As well as meals in the garden, it is perfect for picnics, in which case take some fresh basil leaves wrapped in cling film (plastic wrap) with which to decorate the salad just before serving.

SERVES 4

175 g (6 oz) green pasta twists
75 g (3 oz) mangetout (snow peas), trimmed
6 cauliflower florets, very finely sliced
3 spring onions (scallions), trimmed and finely sliced
small handful fresh basil leaves
15 ml (1 tbsp) finely chopped fresh parsley
75 g (3 oz) fresh Parmesan cheese, cut into small cubes
75 ml (5 tbsp) Garlic Vinaigrette (see page 118)
fresh basil leaves, to garnish

1 Cook the pasta in boiling, salted water for 5–8 minutes until al dente. Drain and cool immediately under running cold water.

2 Steam the mangetout (snow peas) for 3 minutes, then cool them under cold running water. Slice them very finely diagonally.

3 Mix all the vegetables with the pasta, and fold in the chopped herbs and cubed cheese. Dress with the Garlic Vinaigrette.

4 Cover the salad with cling film (plastic wrap), and leave to stand in a cool place (not the refrigerator) for a minimum of 5 hours and a maximum of 24 hours, stirring it from time to time.

Illustrated on pages 126–7

MAIN DISHES

CHERVIL SOUFFLÉ-OMELETTE

Chervil is one of summer's blessings, a delicate and utterly distinctive herb which is supreme in egg dishes. Here it adds its unique flavour to an elegant and impressive soufflé omelette.

SERVES 4

4 eggs, separated
75 ml (5 tbsp) single (light) cream
salt and pepper
2.5 ml ($\frac{1}{2}$ tsp) ground ginger
45 ml (3 tbsp) chopped fresh chervil
25 g (1 oz/2 tbsp) butter
30 ml (2 tbsp) olive oil
cornflowers, to garnish (optional)

1 Beat the egg yolks thoroughly in a bowl. Add the cream and beat again. Add salt and pepper to taste and the ginger. Fold in the chervil. Beat the egg whites until very stiff, then fold in.
2 Melt the butter and olive oil together in a large, heavy, shallow pan over a medium heat. Pour in the soufflé mixture and cook until the bottom begins to set, loosening it with a spatula to prevent it from burning. Fold over.

3 Finish in the oven at 220°C/425°F/mark 7 for 2–3 minutes. If possible, scatter a few cornflowers over the omelette to garnish. Serve promptly.

TAGLIATELLE WITH FENNEL

Here, the slightly aniseed flavour of fresh fennel goes perfectly with fresh pasta in a creamy sauce spiked with garlic and pine nuts.

SERVES 6–8

1 large fennel bulb, trimmed and chopped
75 g (3 oz/6 tbsp) butter
2 large garlic cloves, skinned and crushed
5 ml (1 tsp) grated lemon rind
300 ml ($\frac{1}{2}$ pint/1$\frac{1}{4}$ cups) double (heavy) cream
45 ml (3 tbsp) chopped fresh fennel leaves
salt and pepper
grated nutmeg
juice of 1 lemon
350 g (12 oz) fresh plain tagliatelle
350 g (12 oz) fresh green tagliatelle
75 g (3 oz/$\frac{3}{4}$ cup) grated Parmesan cheese
30 ml (2 tbsp) pine nuts, toasted, to garnish

1 Blanch the chopped fennel in a saucepan of boiling water for 2 minutes. Drain.
2 Melt half of the butter in a pan and gently cook the garlic for 2–3 minutes. Add the blanched fennel and grated lemon rind and cook gently for 3 minutes.
3 Add the remaining butter and the cream and bring almost to the boil. Stir in the fennel leaves and add salt, pepper, nutmeg and lemon juice to taste.
4 Meanwhile, cook the two types of tagliatelle in boiling, salted water until al dente. Drain the pasta and place in a warm serving dish.
5 Spoon half of the hot fennel sauce over the pasta. Add 25 g (1 oz/$\frac{1}{4}$ cup) of the Parmesan cheese, and toss until the sauce coats the pasta. Garnish with the pine nuts and pass around the rest of the sauce along with the remaining Parmesan.

ABOVE: *Focaccia alla Caprese (this page)*

FOCACCIA ALLA CAPRESE

Focaccia, that delicious Italian flat bread available from Italian delicatessens, makes ideal picnic food. One of my favourite ways of serving it is *alla caprese*, as it is known all over Italy. Simple but sublime.

focaccia bread
ripe tomatoes, sliced
mozzarella cheese, sliced
chopped fresh basil
olive oil
basil sprig, to garnish

1 Lay slices of ripe tomato over the bread. Cover with slices of mozzarella cheese.
2 Sprinkle some chopped fresh basil over the cheese, then dribble a little olive oil over.
3 Garnish with a basil sprig.

CHUNKY CHICKEN PATTIES

These mouthwatering patties make a delicious lunch, enjoyed outside on a fine summer's day. You could serve the patties with buttered rice and a tossed salad made with lots of fresh herbs. Miniature Chicken Patties are also delicious; simply make the patties half the usual size, and serve as finger food with drinks.

SERVES 4

450 g (1 lb/2 cups) cooked chicken, chopped
2.5 ml ($\frac{1}{2}$ tsp) garam masala (see page 9) (optional)
50 g (2 oz/$\frac{1}{2}$ cup) Cheddar cheese, finely grated
3 egg yolks

flour, for coating
vegetable oil, for frying
FOR THE BÉCHAMEL SAUCE
½ oz (15 g/1 tbsp) butter
7.5 ml (1½ tsp) plain (all-purpose) flour
75 ml (5 tbsp) milk, heated
salt and pepper

1 To make the Béchamel Sauce, melt the butter in a small saucepan. Stir in the flour and cook over a low heat for 2–3 minutes, stirring constantly. Remove from the heat and gradually add the milk, stirring all the time. Return to the heat and continue stirring until the sauce thickens. Add salt and pepper to taste and simmer over a low heat for 5 minutes.

2. Mix the chicken, garam masala if you are using it, cheese and egg yolks together thoroughly. Blend to a thick paste with the Béchamel Sauce in a food processor or blender.

3 Shape the mixture into 12 small patty shapes and dip in flour.

4 Fry in hot, shallow oil until golden on both sides. Drain on paper towels and serve hot.

PICNIC OMELETTE
FINES HERBES

A cold, lightly spiced omelette *fines herbes* makes perfect picnic fare as a filling for a rolled-up chapati— a thin, flat, unleavened bread from India. Or, if chapatis are not available, soft baps (buns) can be used instead. The omelette is also very good cut into slices and served as finger food with drinks.

MAKES 4

4 eggs
pinch of garam masala (see page 9) or curry powder
salt and pepper
45 ml (3 tbsp) milk
15 g (½ oz/1 tbsp) butter
30 ml (2 tbsp) finely chopped fresh summer herbs,
such as parsley, chives, tarragon and chervil—or other
herbs of your choice
4 chapatis or soft baps (buns)

1 Beat the eggs with the curry powder or garam masala, and some salt and pepper. Beat in the milk.

2 Grease a heavy, shallow pan with the butter. Make 4 thin omelettes the same size as the chapatis, cooking them one at a time. Sprinkle the chopped herbs over each, fold in half, remove from the pan and cool.

3 To assemble, place each omelette on a chapati and fold it in half. If desired, roll it over once more. Pack in cling film (plastic wrap) ready for the picnic.

MUSSELS AND
PASTA TWISTS
WITH BASIL

A stylish dish for an alfresco lunch, this mussel and pasta salad is dressed with a mixture of crème fraîche, raspberry vinegar and fresh basil.

SERVES 4

1.1 litres (2 pints/5 cups) fresh mussels
4 spring onions (scallions), trimmed and finely
chopped
50 ml (2 fl oz/¼ cup) white wine
30 ml (2 tbsp) chopped fresh parsley
225 g (8 oz) pasta twists
100 g (4 oz/½ cup) crème fraîche (see page 10)
small bunch of fresh basil, chopped
30 ml (2 tbsp) raspberry vinegar
red bergamot flowers, to garnish (optional)

1 Scrub the mussels well and remove the beards. Discard any which do not close when tapped.

2 Put the mussels into a large saucepan with the spring onions (scallions), wine and parsley, and cover with a lid. Shake from time to time over a gentle heat for 5–7 minutes until all the mussels have opened.

3 Cool, then remove the mussels from their shells, discarding any that have not opened. Strain the liquid through muslin (cheesecloth) and reserve it.

4 Cook the pasta in a pan of boiling, salted water for 5–8 minutes until al dente. Drain, then rinse the pasta under cold running water to remove the starch.

5 Mix 45–60 ml (3–4 tbsp) of the mussel liquid into the crème fraîche in a bowl. Fold in the basil and raspberry vinegar.

6 Fold in the flavoured crème fraîche, add the mussels and mix. Keep cool, but not chilled, until ready to serve. Garnish with bergamot flowers if available.

CREAMY GINGER CHICKEN

A delicately aromatic chicken dish for a special summer lunch alfresco. You can use either chicken legs or breasts, so long as they are a reasonable size. Serve it with noodles, some mangetout (snow peas) or French beans (green beans), and a salad.

SERVES 6

6 large chicken pieces
salt and pepper
bunch of watercress, trimmed
100 g (4 oz/1 cup) fresh ginger root, peeled and grated
30 ml (2 tbsp) olive oil
450 g (1 lb/2 cups) crème fraîche (see page 10)
4 spring onions (scallions), trimmed and very finely chopped

1 Season the chicken pieces with salt and pepper.
2 Blend the watercress with the ginger and olive oil in a food processor or blender, and spread over chicken. Steam for 20–30 minutes until cooked through.
3 Remove the chicken pieces and place them in a warm serving dish. Stir the cooking juices into the crème fraîche and fold in the spring onions (scallions). Without heating it, spoon the sauce over the warm chicken and serve.

What wondrous life is this I lead!
Ripe apples drop about my head;
The luscious clusters of the vine
Upon my mouth do crush their wine;
The nectarine and curious peach
Into my hands themselves do reach;
Stumbling on melons, as I pass,
Ensnared with flowers, I fall on grass.
Andrew Marvell: "The Garden"

LEFT: *Creamy Ginger Chicken (this page) and Tomato Salad with Tarragon (page 119)*

DESSERTS

INDIVIDUAL SUMMER PUDDINGS

Summer pudding is one of England's great culinary inventions, a beautiful dish of seasonal soft fruits encased in juice-drenched bread. Yet it is beguilingly easy to make. This version, with Raspberry Sauce, makes quite an impression, as each guest is served with a pudding. It needs to be made the day before.

SERVES 6

100 g (4 oz/1 cup) fresh black currants, stalks removed
100 g (4 oz/1 cup) fresh red currants, stalks removed
225 g (8 oz/1½ cups) raspberries, hulls removed
350 g (12 oz/3 cups) cherries, stoned (pitted) and halved
75 ml (5 tbsp) water
45 ml (3 tbsp) caster (superfine) sugar
10–12 slices of white bread
crème fraîche (see page 10), to serve

FOR THE RASPBERRY SAUCE
900 g (2 lb/6 cups) raspberries, hulls removed
50 g (2 oz/½ cup) icing (confectioners') sugar, sifted

1 Reserve a few of the fruits to garnish. Place the rest in a large saucepan with the water. Bring to simmering point over a gentle heat, stirring, and simmer gently for 5 minutes. Stir in the sugar. Cool.

2 Grease 6 individual pudding basins (pudding molds). Trim the crusts from the bread. Cut some of the slices in half lengthwise and line the sides of the basins. Cut more of the slices into circles and line the base of each basin, making sure the edges fit neatly.

3 Fill with the fruit and enough of the juices to just moisten the bread. Cover the top with another circle of bread and moisten with a little juice.

4 Place a small flat plate on top which fits just inside the rim of each basin, and weigh it down with something heavy. Chill overnight.

5 To make the Raspberry Sauce, put the raspberries into a food processor or blender with the sugar, and blend. Pass through a sieve to strain off the pips (seeds). Check for sweetness, adding sugar if necessary.

6 To serve, invert the puddings on to plates, and pour the Raspberry Sauce over. Garnish with the reserved fruits. Serve with crème fraîche.

LIGHT MINT ICE CREAM

Ice cream made with crème fraîche is refreshingly light. Fresh mint gives this ice cream its distinctive, clean flavour which is ideal for summer.

SERVES 6–8

8 small young mint sprigs, taken from top of stem
75 ml (5 tbsp) caster (superfine) sugar
350 ml (12 fl oz/1½ cups) crème fraîche (see page 10)
3 egg whites, stiffly beaten

1 Chop the mint leaves very finely, then put into a blender with the sugar. Blend until well mixed.

2 Stir the sugar and mint mixture into the crème fraîche. Fold in the egg whites. Put into a freezer container and freeze for at least 4 hours.

RIGHT: Individual Summer Puddings (this page)

BLACKBERRY SORBET

A perfect way to eat freshly picked blackberries, this brilliantly coloured sorbet makes a light, refreshing dessert for an alfresco lunch or dinner.

SERVES 6

550 g (1¼ lb) fresh blackberries
60 ml (4 tbsp) water
100 g (4 oz/½ cup) caster (superfine) sugar
300 ml (½ pint/1¼ cups) water
finely grated rind and juice of 1 lemon
2 egg whites, stiffly beaten

1 Reserve some of the blackberries for a garnish, and cook the remainder in 60 ml (4 tbsp) water for about ten minutes until soft. Push through a sieve to purée.
2 Dissolve the sugar in the remaining water over low heat. Add the grated lemon rind and boil for 10 minutes. Cool for 1 hour.
3 Add the lemon juice to the cooled syrup. Strain into a bowl. Stir the blackberry purée into the syrup. Pour into a shallow freezer container and place in the freezer for 3 hours.
4 Remove from the freezer and transfer to a chilled basin. Break the mixture up with a fork, then fold in the beaten egg whites. Return to the freezer and leave for a further 3 hours.
5 About 30 minutes before serving, place the sorbet in the refrigerator to soften. To serve, spoon into dishes. Garnish with the reserved blackberries.

'Tis not through envy of thy happy lot,
But being too happy in thine happiness—
That thou, light-wingèd Dryad of the trees,
In some melodious plot
Of beechen green, and shadows numberless,
Singest of summer in full-throated ease.
John Keats: "Ode to a Nightingale"

RIGHT: *Blackberry Sorbet (this page)*

CHAPTER FOUR

Afternoon Teas

Afternoon tea, a great institution, is particularly delightful outdoors on a fine afternoon. Traditionally, it starts with dainty sandwiches, which are followed by buttered scones, muffins or teabread, and finally cakes and pastries. As an alternative to the classic afternoon tea served at a table in the garden, you could put the tea in a thermos flask, pack some milk, lemon slices and sugar separately, and turn teatime into a proper picnic.

MENU SUGGESTIONS

MENU 17
Cucumber Sandwiches à la Ritz page 60
Chocolate Roulade page 68
lemon verbena or chamomile tea

•

MENU 18
English Country House Scones page 63, *served with Strawberry*
Jam page 63
Lemon Tart page 67
Earl Grey or jasmine tea

•

MENU 19
All-American Muffins page 60
Creamy Peach Gâteau page 70
Assam or peppermint tea

•

MENU 20
Oat and Sesame Crunch page 64
Danish Apple Cake page 67
Darjeeling or rose-hip tea

•

MENU 21
Almond Cookies page 64
Chocolate Walnut Brownies page 68
Lapsang Souchong or orange blossom tea

SANDWICHES & BREADS

CUCUMBER SANDWICHES À LA RITZ

Tea at the Ritz in London's busy Piccadilly is an experience to treasure. The Edwardian decor, the formal service, the live music by a small band in the Palm Court—all help to make tea at this lovely old hotel quite unique. Their sandwiches are superb—very fresh, cut extremely thinly, using both brown and white bread. The English cucumber sandwich *par excellence*, perfect for teatime in the garden in high summer.

fresh brown bread, thinly sliced
fresh white bread, thinly sliced
softened unsalted butter
cucumber, peeled and very thinly sliced
salt

1 Remove the crusts from the bread. Spread one side with butter.
2 Pat the slices of cucumber dry on paper towels. Lay them on the buttered sides of half of the bread so that they overlap. Sprinkle with a very little salt. Sandwich with the rest of the bread.
3 Cut each sandwich into quarters, and serve them as fresh as possible.

ALL-AMERICAN MUFFINS

A batch of home-baked muffins, fresh from the oven, is one of life's pleasures. Serve them with butter and some Fresh Strawberry Jam (see page 63).

MAKES 10

100 g (4 oz/1 cup) plain (all-purpose) flour
15 ml (1 tbsp) baking powder
pinch of salt
100 g (4 oz/$\frac{2}{3}$ cup) cornmeal
50 g 2 oz/3 tbsp) clear honey
50 g (2 oz/$\frac{1}{2}$ cup) raisins or fresh red currants
60 ml (4 tbsp) sunflower oil
75–100 ml (3–4 fl oz/$\frac{1}{3}$–$\frac{1}{2}$ cup) water

1 Grease a baking sheet. Sift the flour with the baking powder and salt into a bowl. Stir in the cornmeal. Mix in the honey, fruit, sunflower oil and water, then beat to a batter-like consistency.
2 Knead the dough on a lightly floured surface until smooth and light. Roll out to 1 cm ($\frac{1}{2}$ inch) thickness. Cut into 7.5 cm (3 inch) circles, using a large glass as a cutter, and place on the prepared baking sheet.
3 Bake at 180°C/350°F/mark 4 for 15–20 minutes until risen and golden. Serve warm.

Soon will the high Midsummer pomps come on,
Soon will the musk carnations break and swell,
Soon shall we have gold-dusted snap-dragon,
Sweet-William with his homely cottage-smell,
And stocks in fragrant blow;
Roses that down the alleys shine afar,
And open, jasmine-muffled lattices,
And groups under the dreaming garden-trees,
And the full moon, and the white evening-star.
Matthew Arnold: "Thyrsis"

STRAWBERRY JAM

One of my favourite summer expeditions is to go strawberry-picking, to gather enough strawberries to make jam to last us till autumn. This engagingly simple jam has an incomparably fresh and fruity flavour. Enjoy it with the Scones on this page, with the All-American Muffins on page 60—or simply with fresh bread still warm from the oven. You can use ordinary granulated sugar for the jam, but preserving sugar (a coarse type of granulated sugar) is preferable because the large white crystals dissolve slowly, creating less froth. Jam made with preserving sugar also does not have to be stirred so often.

MAKES 1.4–1.8 kg (3–4 lb)

1.4 kg (3 lb) strawberries, hulls removed
900 g (2 lb/4 cups) preserving or granulated sugar
1 thick slice of lemon
150 ml ($\frac{1}{4}$ pint/$\frac{2}{3}$ cup) water

1 Put the strawberries, sugar, lemon and water into a large saucepan. Simmer gently until the sugar has dissolved, then boil rapidly for about 10 minutes, stirring occasionally, until setting point is reached. (To test for set, put a teaspoonful of the jam on to a cold saucer and put in a cold place, drawing the pan of jam off the heat. After 5 minutes, if the jam wrinkles a little and does not run when the saucer is tilted, it is ready. If it is not ready, continue boiling. Test every few minutes until setting point is reached.)
2 Leave to settle for a few minutes, then lift off any scum with a slotted spoon.
3 Pot in warm, clean jars and seal immediately. Store in a cool place. Use within 6 weeks.

Breathless, we flung us on the windy hill,
Laughed in the sun, and kissed the lovely grass.
Rupert Brooke: "The Hill"

LEFT (clockwise from top): *English Country House Scones (this page), All-American Muffins (page 60), Strawberry Jam (this page), Cucumber Sandwiches à la Ritz (page 60)*

I saw an arbour with a drooping roof
Of trellis vines, and bells, and larger blooms,
Like floral censers, swinging light in air;
Before its wreathèd doorway, on a mound
Of moss, was spread a feast of summer fruits
John Keats: "The Fall of Hyperion"

ENGLISH COUNTRY HOUSE SCONES

No English country house tea is complete without freshly baked scones. On one visit to a stately home, I sampled the best scones I had ever had. Afterwards, I spent some time experimenting to find a recipe to match them. This is it. These scones are fantastic: light, crumbly and with a lovely texture and flavour. They always work beautifully—and they freeze very well, too. They are irresistible with Strawberry Jam (see this page).

MAKES 12

350 g (12 oz/3 cups) plain (all-purpose) flour
20 ml (4 tsp) baking powder
40 g (1$\frac{1}{2}$ oz/3 tbsp) caster (superfine) sugar
50 g (2 oz/$\frac{1}{4}$ cup) spreadable margarine
1 egg
125–150 ml (4–5 fl oz/$\frac{1}{2}$–$\frac{2}{3}$ cup) milk
beaten egg mixed with 30 ml (2 tbsp) milk, for glazing

1 Lightly grease a baking sheet. Sift the dry ingredients together into a bowl. Rub in the margarine lightly with your fingertips until the mixture resembles fine breadcrumbs.
2 Beat the egg with half of the milk and mix into the dry ingredients, then add more milk as you beat, to bring to a soft dough.
3 Lightly knead the dough on a floured surface. Roll out to 2 cm ($\frac{3}{4}$ inch) thick. Cut the dough into 6.5 cm (2$\frac{1}{2}$ inch) circles with a cutter and place on the prepared baking sheet. Brush with beaten egg and milk glaze.
4 Bake at 220°C/425°F/mark 7 for 10 minutes or until well risen and golden.

CAKES, TARTS & COOKIES

OAT AND SESAME CRUNCH

These crunchy oat and sesame squares are the perfect answer for a picnic tea, as they are not only wholesome and delicious, but they also travel well, wrapped in cling film (plastic wrap). Use clear honey, which has been heat-treated and therefore blends and dissolves more easily than the thicker, untreated type.

MAKES 12

175 g (6 oz/¾ cup) spreadable margarine
75 ml (5 tbsp) clear honey
250 g (9 oz/3 cups) fine or medium whole-grain oats
50 g (2 oz/⅓ cup) sesame seeds

1 Thoroughly grease a 20.5 cm (8 inch) square cake tin (pan). Melt the margarine with the honey in a saucepan.
2 Mix the oats with the sesame seeds and pour in the melted margarine mixture. Mix thoroughly. Press the oat mixture into the prepared tin.
3 Bake at 180°C/350°F/mark 4 for 20–25 minutes. Leave to cool for 15 minutes, then mark into squares with a knife, without actually cutting right through. Lift out when cold, separating them into squares along the marked lines.

ALMOND COOKIES

Sophisticated, light and crisp, these almond cookies turn a picnic into a feast. They freeze well, too.

MAKES 16

100 g (4 oz/1 cup) flaked (slivered) almonds
150 g (5 oz/½ cup plus 2 tbsp) caster (superfine) sugar
100 g (4 oz/1 cup) plain (all-purpose) flour
10 ml (2 tsp) baking powder
100 g (4 oz/½ cup) butter or margarine, melted

1 Grease a baking sheet. Place the nuts on another baking sheet. Toast at 190°C/375°F/mark 5 for 10 minutes, shaking the sheet from time to time. Cool.
2 Grind half of the toasted nuts with half of the sugar, then put into a bowl. Stir in the flour, the rest of the sugar and the baking powder. Mix well.
3 Stir the browned almonds into the mixture with the melted butter. Knead lightly until thoroughly blended.
4 Roll teaspoons of the mixture to a round, flattish shape with your hands. Place on the baking sheet.
5 Bake at 190°C/375°F/mark 5 for 10 minutes until golden brown. Store in airtight containers.

July, who scatters from his pockets
The fluff of blow-balls in a cloud,
Who enters through the open window,
Who chatters to himself aloud,
Unkempt, untidy, absent-minded,
Soaked through with smell of dill and rye,
With linden-blossom, grass and beet-leaves,
The meadow-scented month July.
Boris Pasternak: "July"

RIGHT: *Almond Cookies (this page)*

DANISH APPLE CAKE

This cake has a superb texture, and the flavour of the apples is unbeatable. The spices add a delightful pungency and aroma. Serve this cake for a special occasion, and pass around thick Greek yogurt to go with it. It needs to be eaten with a spoon!

SERVES 6

100 g (4 oz) spreadable margarine
100 g (4 oz/$\frac{2}{3}$ cup) soft light brown sugar
2 eggs
25 g (1 oz/$\frac{1}{4}$ cup) plain (all-purpose) flour
75 g (3 oz/$\frac{3}{4}$ cup) ground almonds
5 ml (1 tsp) baking powder
45 ml (3 tbsp) milk
5 ml (1 tsp) almond extract
FOR THE FILLING
900 g (2 lb) Bramleys (tart green apples), cored and sliced (7 cups, prepared volume)
30 ml (2 tbsp) apple juice
100 g (4 oz/$\frac{1}{2}$ cup) raw cane sugar
4 cloves
5 ml (1 tsp) ground mixed spice (nutmeg, cinnamon, cloves and allspice)
50 g (2 oz/$\frac{1}{3}$ cup) raisins
TO DECORATE
toasted flaked (slivered) almonds
icing (confectioners') sugar, sifted

1 Grease a 20.5 cm (8 inch) square cake tin (pan). Cream the margarine with the sugar in a bowl and beat in the eggs. Fold in the flour and ground almonds, then mix in the baking powder.
2 Beat in the milk until the mixture is smooth. Add the almond extract. Put the mixture into the prepared cake tin.
3 Bake at 180°C/350°F/mark 4 for 30 minutes. Cool on a wire rack, then slice into two layers.
4 Meanwhile, prepare the apple filling. Place the apples, apple juice, sugar and cloves in a saucepan and cook for about 5–8 minutes until soft and pulpy. Add the mixed spice and raisins. Cool.
5 Spread half of the mixture over the bottom half of

LEFT: Lemon Tart (this page)

the cake. Place the other layer on top, and spread the rest of the apple mixture over the top. Sprinkle with a little icing (confectioners') sugar and the toasted almonds just before serving.

LEMON TART

An exceptional tart with all the freshness of lemon and a biscuit crust (graham cracker crust) as its base. Every time I make this, someone asks me for the recipe, so here it is. Enjoy it for a summer's tea laid in the garden, as you bask in the afternoon sun.

SERVES 4–6

FOR THE CRUST
225 g (8 oz) digestive biscuits (graham crackers)
30 ml (2 tbsp) caster (superfine) sugar
75 g (3 oz/6 tbsp) butter or margarine, melted
FOR THE LEMON FILLING
2 large lemons
100 g (4 oz/$\frac{1}{2}$ cup) caster (superfine) sugar
3 eggs
50 g (2 oz/$\frac{1}{4}$ cup) butter, melted

1 Thoroughly grease a 20.5 cm (8 inch) flan tin (pie pan).
2 To make the crust, break up the biscuits (graham crackers) and put them into a food processor or blender. Blend to fine crumbs.
3 Mix the crumbs with the sugar and stir in the melted butter or margarine until well blended.
4 Press into the prepared flan tin. Chill while preparing the lemon filling.
5 Carefully cut 3 long strips of rind from one of the lemons and then cut them into long narrow shreds. Simmer the shredded lemon rind in water to cover for 5–7 minutes until tender. Drain, toss in half the sugar and set aside.
6 Grate the remaining rinds on the fine side of the grater. Squeeze the juice from the lemons, then strain. Mix together and beat in the eggs, the remaining sugar and the melted butter. Pour into the prepared flan case (pie crust).
7 Bake at 180°C/350°F/mark 4 for 25 minutes. Cool in the tin. Arrange the shreds of peel over the top of the tart. Serve chilled.

CHOCOLATE WALNUT BROWNIES

When children are around for teatime, a batch of these brownies disappears all too quickly! Rich and chocolatey, with an added crunch of walnuts, they make a special occasion of an alfresco tea.

MAKES 16

3 eggs
150 g (5 oz/¾ cup) soft light brown sugar
5 ml (1 tsp) vanilla extract
pinch of salt
225 g (8 oz/1⅓ cups) plain (semisweet) chocolate, chopped
100 g (4 oz/½ cup) butter or margarine
100 g (4 oz/1 cup) self-raising flour (or, in the U.S.,
1 cup all-purpose flour plus ¼ tsp baking powder)
25 g (1 oz/¼ cup) walnuts, chopped
75 ml (5 tbsp) double (heavy) cream

1 Grease a 20.5 cm (8 inch) square cake tin (pan). Beat the eggs with the sugar in a bowl until pale and creamy. Beat in the vanilla and salt.
2 Melt 150 g (5 oz) of the chocolate with the butter, then stir into the mixture. Fold in the flour and then the walnuts. Mix well. Pour into the prepared cake tin.
3 Bake at 180°C/350°F/mark 4 for 15–18 minutes or until a knife inserted in the centre comes out clean.
4 Put the cream into a small, heavy pan and bring to

And August comes, when fields are sere and brown,
When stubble takes the place of ruffling corn;
When the sweet grass is like a prisoner shorn;
The air is full of drifting thistledown,
Grey pointed sprites, that on the breezes ride.
The cloyed trees droop, the ash-keys spinning fall;
The brooks are pebbly, for the trickle's dried;
Birds moult, and in the leafy copses hide,
And summer makes a silence after spring,
As who with age a liberal youth should chide.
Vita Sackville-West: "The Land"

the boil. Remove from the heat and stir in the remaining chocolate. Stir until it melts.
5 Pour the chocolate cream over the cooked cake in the tin and smooth down. Leave to set. Cut into squares and lift out carefully.

CHOCOLATE ROULADE

This soft, dark chocolate roulade, rolled up with crème fraîche inside, is succulent and tempting. The texture is smooth, the taste rich and lasting.

SERVES 4–6

5 eggs, separated
175 g (6 oz/1 cup) soft light brown sugar
45 ml (3 tbsp) hot water
175 g (6 oz/1 cup) plain (semisweet) chocolate, melted
TO FINISH
icing (confectioners') sugar, sifted
crème fraîche (see page 10)
grated white chocolate

1 Grease and line a 25.5 × 35.5 cm (10 × 14 inch) Swiss roll tin (jelly roll pan) with greased greaseproof (waxed) paper.
2 Put the egg yolks into a bowl and beat with the sugar until pale and creamy.
3 Stir the hot water into the melted chocolate, and stir this into the egg yolk mixture. Beat the whites until very stiff and fold them in.
4 Pour the chocolate mixture into the prepared tin.
5 Bake at 200°C/400°F/mark 6 for 15 minutes. Leave to cool in the tin for 10 minutes, then cover with a damp clean cloth and leave for a further 10 minutes.
6 Turn out on to a piece of greaseproof (waxed) paper lightly dusted with icing (confectioners') sugar. Peel off the lining paper and leave to cool completely.
7 Spread with some of the crème fraîche sweetened with icing sugar to taste. Roll up carefully from one end, using the paper to help. Decorate with the chocolate and sugar. Cut into slices and serve accompanied by more crème fraîche if desired.

RIGHT: *Chocolate Roulade (this page)*

CREAMY PEACH GÂTEAU

Fresh peaches are one of the great delights of summer, and their texture goes perfectly with a light sponge cake filled with crème fraîche.

SERVES 6–8

4 eggs
100 g (4 oz/$\frac{1}{2}$ cup) caster (superfine) sugar
100 g (4 oz/1 cup) plain (all-purpose) flour
pinch of salt
FOR THE FILLING AND TOPPING
2 peaches
225 g (8 oz/1 cup) crème fraîche (see page 10)
icing (confectioners') sugar

1 Grease and line 2 shallow 18 cm (7 inch) sandwich tins (round layer cake pans) with greased greaseproof (waxed) paper.
2 Beat the eggs with the sugar very thoroughly in a bowl until pale, creamy and thick.
3 Sift the flour and salt over the top and fold in gently with a metal spoon. Pour into the prepared tins.
4 Bake at 180°C/350°F/mark 4 for 30–35 minutes until they shrink from the sides and are spongy in the centre.
5 Cool in the tins for 5 minutes, then turn out on to a wire rack. Peel off the lining paper and cool.
6 To make the filling and topping, pour boiling water over the peaches and leave for 1 minute. Skin, then cut them in half and remove the stones (pits). Slice thinly.
7 Sweeten the crème fraîche to taste with icing (confectioners') sugar. Spread one-third of this on to the bottom of one of the cakes. Cover with half of the peaches and spread the same amount again over the fruit. Cover with the second cake, spread with the remaining crème fraîche, then decorate with the rest of the peach slices.

. . . two hundred loaves of bread, and an hundred bunches of raisins, and an hundred of summer fruits, and a bottle of wine.
The Bible: 2 Sam. 16: 1

CHAPTER FIVE

Evening Drinks and Dips

Drinks out-of-doors on balmy evenings are one of the joys of summertime. Exotic wine cups and fruit punches add a celebratory touch yet are not too high in alcohol; accompany them with a variety of summery dips and nibbles. You can set out the glasses on a table on the lawn or the patio. On cooler evenings, a conservatory or sunporch provides a pleasant setting, the doors opening out on to the garden to make the most of the lingering warmth.

MENU SUGGESTIONS

MENU 22
Tea Punch page 79
Picnic Omelette Fines Herbes page 49, *sliced*

•

MENU 23
Borage Fruit Cup with White Wine page 76
Minty Yogurt Dip page 86, *served with pitta bread strips and crudités*

•

MENU 24
Chilled Wine Cup with Mint page 79
Filo Party Pieces page 82

•

MENU 25
Rosemary Claret Cup page 76
Cheese Straws with Sesame page 85

•

MENU 26
Peach Shake page 80
Guacamole Tacos page 82

•

MENU 27
Mint Julep page 79
Herbed Olives page 86
Sesame Cheese Crumbles page 82

•

MENU 28
Elderflower Champagne page 80
Spiced Aubergine (Eggplant) Dip page 83, *served with pitta bread strips and crudités*

ALCOHOLIC DRINKS

ROSEMARY CLARET CUP

In this drink, oranges and lemons are marinated in red wine. The famous herb liqueur, chartreuse, along with some fresh rosemary and lemon thyme, adds an exotic flavour. Lemon thyme has softer leaves than ordinary garden thyme, and a delicate lemon fragrance well suited to a summer evening.

SERVES 4–6

75 cl (25 fl oz) bottle claret or Cabernet Sauvignon
25 ml (1 fl oz) chartreuse
juice of 2 oranges
juice of 1 lemon
3 rosemary sprigs
$\frac{1}{4}$ medium cucumber, thinly sliced
lemon thyme sprigs
15 ml (1 tbsp) caster (superfine) sugar
600 ml (1 pint/2$\frac{1}{2}$ cups) soda water, chilled
mallow flowers, to decorate (optional)

1 Put all the ingredients, except the soda water, into a large bowl or jug (pitcher). Chill thoroughly for several hours.
2 Just before serving, add the soda water and float mallow flowers on top if available.
Illustrated on pages 84–5

BORAGE FRUIT CUP WITH WHITE WINE

The Ancient Greeks steeped the herb borage in wine to dispel melancholy, and this wine cup, garnished with sliced fruit and bright blue borage flowers, does indeed lift the spirits—particularly on a lovely summer's evening.

SERVES 12

2.3 litres (4 pints/2$\frac{1}{2}$ quarts) white wine, chilled
250 ml (8 fl oz/1 cup) crème de cassis (blackcurrant liqueur)
1 litre (1$\frac{3}{4}$ pints/1 quart) tropical fruit juice, chilled
600 ml (1 pint/2$\frac{1}{2}$ cups) sparkling mineral water, chilled
TO DECORATE
borage flowers
sliced fresh fruit, such as apple, orange, cherries, strawberries, kiwi fruit

1 Mix the white wine with the crème de cassis in a large jug (pitcher). Add the tropical juice and chill.
2 Just before serving, pour in the sparkling mineral water. Decorate the top with sprigs of borage and slices of fresh fruit.

Now summer is in flower and natures hum
Is never silent round her sultry bloom
Insects as small as dust are never done
Wi' glittering dance and reeling in the sun
And green wood fly and blossom haunting bee
Are never weary of their melody
Round field hedge now flowers in full glory twine
Large bindweed bells wild hop and streakd woodbine
That lift athirst their slender throated flowers
Agape for dew falls and for honey showers
John Clare: "The Shepherd's Calendar"

MINT JULEP

This famous drink, traditionally served in a small silver goblet, is both refreshing and stimulating. Linger over it as you sit in the sunshine of a midsummer's evening before dinner at dusk. It is lovely with the Herbed Olives on page 86.

SERVES 1

5–10 ml (1–2 tsp) caster (superfine) sugar
5–10 ml (1–2 tsp) water
crushed ice or ice cubes
6 mint leaves
50–100 ml (2–4 fl oz) bourbon
1 mint sprig, dipped in icing (confectioners') sugar

1 Dissolve the sugar in the water in a saucepan over low heat. Bring it to the boil, then remove from the heat, and cool.
2 Half-fill a chilled glass or goblet with crushed ice, or ice cubes if preferred. Add the sugar syrup, mint leaves and bourbon. Stir vigorously with a wooden spoon to crush the mint leaves.
3 Decorate with the frosted mint sprig.

CHILLED WINE CUP WITH MINT

Quick and easy to make, this wine cup is perfect for a celebratory drink on the patio early in the evening—at the time when night-scented stocks and honeysuckle begin to give out their sweet fragrance. Mint is a classic garnish for wine cups and makes a refreshing drink in hot weather.

SERVES 8

sliced fresh fruit, such as strawberries, apple, seedless grapes, orange
1 litre (1¾ pints/1 quart) dry white wine, chilled
600 ml (1 pint/2½ cups) fizzy lemonade (lemon soda)
crushed ice
8 small mint sprigs

LEFT (from left to right): Mint Julep (this page), Tea Punch (this page)

1 Prepare the fruit and place in a large bowl. Pour over the chilled wine and lemonade (lemon soda).
2 Stir in the crushed ice and ladle into glasses. Serve with a sprig of mint in each glass.

TEA PUNCH

This non-alcoholic punch makes a delicious refresher on a hot day. The term "punch" is thought to have come from the Hindu name for a drink made from tea, water, sugar, citrus juice and spirit, which was enjoyed by the British raj in India.

MAKES 1.7 litres (3 pints/7½ cups)

1.1 litres (2 pints/5 cups) boiling water
15 ml (3 tsp) Earl Grey tea leaves
honey to taste
juice of 6 oranges
slices of lime
small handful of mint leaves
150 ml (¼ pint/⅔ cup) brandy
ice cubes
mint sprigs, to garnish

1 Pour the boiling water over the tea leaves in a teapot, and infuse for 4–5 minutes.
2 Strain off the tea and sweeten to taste with honey.
3 Stir in the orange juice, lime slices, mint leaves and brandy, and chill thoroughly.
4 To serve, pour over ice in tall glasses, garnishing each with a sprig of mint.

PEACH SHAKE

A truly marvellous summer celebration drink, in
which the taste of peach predominates. Decorate it
with exotic hibiscus flowers, if you have them.

SERVES 4

300 ml ($\frac{1}{2}$ pint/$1\frac{1}{4}$ cups) sweet white wine, such as
Muscat de Venise, chilled
6 ripe peaches, stoned (pitted), peeled and chopped
90 ml (6 tbsp) icing (confectioners') sugar
crushed ice
hawthorn or hibiscus flowers, to decorate (optional)

1 Blend the wine, peaches and sugar in a food
processor or blender at high speed for about $\frac{1}{2}$ minute.
2 Pour the drink into champagne flutes over crushed
ice. Decorate with flowers if available.

ELDERFLOWER CHAMPAGNE

Elderflowers give drinks a delicate and unique
flavour, reminiscent of their scent on the tree on a
sunny day. This "champagne" is one of the highlights
of midsummer, redolent of flowers and sunshine.

MAKES 5.7 LITRES (5 quarts/$24\frac{1}{2}$ cups)

4.5 litres (4 quarts/5 quarts) boiling water
550 g ($1\frac{1}{4}$ lb/$2\frac{1}{2}$ cups) granulated sugar
2 large lemons, thickly sliced
30 ml (2 tbsp) white wine vinegar
8 heads of elderflowers
rose petals, to garnish (optional)

1 Pour the boiling water over all the ingredients in a
large bowl. Stir well until the sugar dissolves. Leave to
stand, covered, in a warm place for 24 hours.
2 Strain off, then decant into clean bottles. Cork, and
leave for about 3 weeks.
3 Serve chilled, in champagne flutes. Scatter a few
rose petals, if available, on top of each glass, removing
the white "heels" first.

RIGHT: *Peach Shake (this page)*

NIBBLES & DIPS

FILO PARTY PIECES

These little morsels make a delectable snack to go with a drink in the cool of the evening. The filo pastry shells are golden, light and crisp, the filling a summery combination of courgette (zucchini) and corn flavoured with garlic and ginger. The pastry shells and the filling can be prepared in advance, then assembled just before serving, if you prefer. There won't be any leftovers.

MAKES 18

FOR THE FILO CUPS
6 sheets of filo pastry, each about 19 × 38 cm
(7½ × 15 inches)
25 g (1 oz/2 tbsp) butter, melted
FOR THE FILLING
3 medium courgettes (zucchini), grated
175 g (6 oz) baby sweetcorn (miniature corncobs),
very finely sliced
2.5 cm (1 inch) fresh ginger root, peeled and finely
grated
1 medium garlic clove, skinned and crushed
60 ml (4 tbsp) crème fraîche (see page 10)
soy sauce, to taste

1 Cut each sheet of filo pastry into 6.5 cm (2½ inch) squares, cutting through all 6 sheets at once, so that you have 18 6-layer sets of squares. Brush each layer with melted butter, and place the sets of squares in tiny patty tins (miniature muffin pans) or *petits fours* tins (pans). Press the pastry layers into the base of each hole, and spread out the edges. Place a ball of crumpled foil inside each one to keep it in place.
2 Bake the pastry shells at 200°C/400°F/mark 6 for 10 minutes, removing the foil balls after 5 minutes. Cool on a wire rack, then lift out carefully.
3 To make the filling, steam the grated courgettes (zucchini) with the corn and ginger for about 3 minutes until softened. Leave until cold.
4 Mix the garlic into the crème fraîche and stir into the vegetables, adding soy sauce to taste.
5 Pile the filling into the filo shells just before serving.

SESAME CHEESE CRUMBLES

These crumbly, cheesy snacks will vanish in no time at all when you serve them with drinks before supper.

MAKES 30

75 g (3 oz/¾ cup) plain (all-purpose) flour
100 g (4 oz/½ cup) spreadable margarine
75 g (3 oz/¾ cup) Cheddar cheese, finely grated
45 ml (3 tbsp) sesame seeds
pinch of salt

1 Thoroughly grease a baking sheet.
2 Blend all the ingredients together in a bowl.
3 Roll the dough into little balls the size of small marbles. Put on to the prepared baking sheet and press down flat.
4 Bake at 190°C/375°F/mark 5 for 10–15 minutes until crisp. Cool on a wire rack.

GUACAMOLE TACOS

A rich, smooth guacamole, lightly spiced, makes an excellent filling for tacos, piled on to a base of crisp salad. Though more than a nibble, these go well with drinks on a summer's evening before a light supper.

SERVES 6–8

1 crisp lettuce, finely shredded
60 ml (4 tbsp) Vinaigrette (see page 42)
12 taco shells
TO GARNISH
small tomato wedges
FOR THE GUACAMOLE
2 very ripe avocados, peeled and stoned (pitted)
30 ml (2 tbsp) lemon juice
2 medium tomatoes, skinned and chopped
chilli powder or garam masala (see page 9), to taste
5 ml (1 tsp) ground coriander
5 ml (1 tsp) salt

1. Blend all the Guacamole ingredients in a food processor or blender. Adjust the seasoning to taste.

2 Toss the shredded lettuce in the Vinaigrette, then put a layer into each taco.

3 Top the lettuce with the Guacamole and garnish with tomato wedges.

SPICED AUBERGINE (EGGPLANT) DIP

Exotic yet easy to make, this dip is ideal for an alfresco drinks party, especially if you are serving one of the wine cups on pages 76–80. Accompany it with pitta bread and a selection of crudités.

SERVES 4

2 medium aubergines (eggplants)
75 ml (5 tbsp) olive oil
30 ml (2 tbsp) tahini (see page 9)
1 large garlic clove, skinned and crushed
15–30 ml (1–2 tbsp) lemon juice
5–10 ml (1–2 tsp) ground cumin
90 ml (6 tbsp) chopped fresh parsley
salt and pepper

TO GARNISH
lettuce leaves
black olives
parsley sprigs

1 Place the whole aubergines (eggplants) in a baking dish. Bake at 180°C/350°F/mark 4 for 25 minutes or until the flesh is soft. Cool completely.

2 Scoop out the flesh and put into a food processor or blender. Add the olive oil, tahini, garlic, lemon juice, cumin and parsley. Blend until quite smooth. Add salt and pepper to taste.

3 Pile the dip into a serving dish lined with lettuce leaves. Garnish with black olives and sprigs of parsley.

Oh! but to breathe the breath
Of the cowslip and primrose sweet—
With the sky above my head,
And the grass beneath my feet;
Thomas Hood: "The Song of the Shirt"

CHEESE STRAWS
WITH SESAME

Passed around with evening drinks, cheese straws always disappear fast. These golden ones, sprinkled with sesame seeds, are especially good. They should be eaten warm and will reheat very well.

MAKES 24

225 g (8 oz) frozen puff pastry, thawed
100 g (4 oz/1 cup) Cheddar cheese, grated
2 egg yolks, beaten
60 ml (4 tbsp) sesame seeds

1 On a floured surface, roll out the puff pastry to a rectangle 5 mm ($\frac{1}{4}$ inch) thick. Sprinkle the grated cheese over one half and fold the other half over the top. Moisten the pastry edges with water and press down firmly, being careful not to trap too much air inside.
2 Roll out again to a large rectangle. Brush with the egg yolk and sprinkle the top thickly with sesame seeds, pressing them down lightly. With a sharp knife, mark into long straws about 5 mm ($\frac{1}{4}$ inch) wide, without cutting right through the pastry.
3 Place on a baking sheet and bake at 220°C/425°F/mark 7 for 15 minutes until well risen and golden. Cool on a wire rack for 5 minutes.
4 Break into straws and eat as soon as possible.

LEFT: *Rosemary Claret Cup (page 76), Cheese Straws with Sesame (this page)*

85

MINTY YOGURT DIP

Yogurt and mint go beautifully together. Add garlic, chives and lemon juice and you have a refreshing and delicious dip that is perfect for a summer celebration. Serve with strips of pitta bread and crudités.

SERVES 4

60 ml (4 tbsp) cottage cheese
60 ml (4 tbsp) plain yogurt
2 mint sprigs, finely chopped
1 garlic clove, skinned and crushed
small bunch of chives, chopped
juice of $\frac{1}{2}$ lemon
salt and pepper
chive flowers, to garnish (optional)

1 Blend the cottage cheese with the yogurt in a food processor or blender until smooth. Add the mint, garlic and chives, then blend again.
2 Stir in the lemon juice and add salt and pepper to taste. Mix thoroughly, and chill. Serve chilled, garnished with chive flowers if available.

HERBED OLIVES

When you are serving evening drinks on the patio, put out a large bowl of these gleaming, aromatic olives for people to nibble. In fact, they are an excellent stand-by to keep in the store cupboard at any time of the year.

black olives
marjoram, rosemary and thyme sprigs
garlic cloves, skinned and thinly sliced
1 or more dried chillies, to taste (optional)
olive oil

1 Put enough black olives into a jar to make it three-quarters full. Add the marjoram, rosemary and thyme and the garlic; add chilli(es) if desired. Fill up the jar with olive oil.
2 Seal the jar and leave the olives to marinate in the oil for at least 2 weeks—the longer you leave it, the better the flavour.
3 Use within 6 months, then use the remaining oil in salad dressings.

CHAPTER SIX

Barbecues

A barbecue is the ultimate alfresco meal, and the distinctive smoky taste of charcoal-grilled food epitomizes the cooking of summer. Meat and poultry, steeped in an aromatic marinade, are traditional barbecue fare, but there are also many wonderful ways of barbecuing fish, vegetables and even fruit. Enjoyed as much for its informality as for the food, a barbecue allows everyone to get involved: there is nothing quite like it.

LEFT: Tangy Shellfish (page 94)

MENU SUGGESTIONS

MENU 29
Vegetable Kebabs page 92
Garlicky Corn on the Cob page 102
Buttery Mushrooms with Coriander page 101
Chinese Carrot Salad page 96
Tomatoes with Blue Cheese and Yogurt Dressing page 100
Barbecued Pears page 104

•

MENU 30
Barbecued Salmon page 92
Marinated Mushroom Kebabs page 97
Leeks in Blue-cheese Dressing page 102
Tossed Salad with Sesame Seed Mayonnaise page 101
Melt-in-the-mouth Bananas page 104

•

MENU 31
Tangy Shellfish page 94
Cheesy Tomatoes page 96
Mixed Salad with Tahini Mayonnaise page 100
Flageolets al Pesto page 96
Fruit Salad on a Stick page 104

MAIN DISHES

VEGETABLE KEBABS

These lightly marinated vegetables make stunning kebabs, with their red, green, purple and mushroom colours alternating on the sticks. They are aromatic with herbs as well as the charcoal flavour.

SERVES 4

1 large aubergine (eggplant), cut into cubes
1 large red pepper, seeded and chopped into 2.5 cm (1 inch) pieces
8 small onions, peeled and blanched
16 small button mushrooms
8 cherry tomatoes
1 medium cucumber, diced coarsely
4 celery sticks, blanched and cut into 2.5 cm (1 inch) pieces
chopped mixed fresh herbs (such as marjoram, oregano, fennel, tarragon, chives), to garnish
FOR THE MARINADE
100 ml (4 fl oz/½ cup) lemon juice
30 ml (2 tbsp) oil
1 garlic clove, skinned and crushed
15 ml (1 tbsp) dried thyme

1 Mix all the marinade ingredients together and leave to stand while preparing the vegetables.

2 Pour the marinade over the prepared vegetables and toss well. Leave to stand for 1–2 hours.
3 Lift out the vegetables, reserving the juices. Thread the vegetables alternately on to skewers.
4 Barbecue on the grill for 10 minutes, until the onions are quite soft, brushing frequently with the marinade. Sprinkle with the herbs just before serving.

BARBECUED SALMON

In this recipe a whole salmon, stuffed with flavoured butter and moistened with wine and lemon juice, is barbecued in foil to keep it succulent.

SERVES 4

100 g (4 oz/½ cup) unsalted butter
20 ml (4 tsp) dried dillweed (dill leaves)
finely grated rind and juice of 1 lemon
salt and pepper
1.5 kg (3 lb) salmon, cleaned
75 ml (3 fl oz) dry white wine
lemon slices and dill sprigs, to garnish

1 Blend the butter with the dill, lemon rind and salt and pepper to taste. Form into a roll, wrap in foil, and chill in the refrigerator for 2–3 hours until firm.
2 Place the fish in the centre of a large piece of foil.
3 Using a sharp knife, cut the flavoured butter into slices. Peel off and discard the foil after cutting.
4 Place the butter slices inside the belly of the fish. Sprinkle the outside of the fish with salt and pepper, then slowly pour over the wine and lemon juice.
5 Fold the foil over the fish to form a loose package so that the wine and juices do not leak out. Place the foil package on the barbecue and grill for 45 minutes. Serve hot, garnished with lemon slices and dill sprigs.

RIGHT (clockwise from top): *Hot Basil Bread (page 133), Vegetable Kebabs (this page), Garlicky Corn on the Cob (page 102)*

TANGY SHELLFISH

For a special occasion, nothing can beat king prawns (jumbo shrimp) cooked on a barbecue after being marinated in lime juice, oil and garlic, to enhance their natural flavour. Serve them simply with wedges of lime, or, if you prefer, with Watercress Mayonnaise.

SERVES 6

24 king prawns (jumbo shrimp) in their shells
juice of 3 limes
2 garlic cloves, skinned and crushed
60 ml (4 tbsp) olive oil
pepper
lime wedges, to garnish (optional)
FOR THE WATERCRESS MAYONNAISE (OPTIONAL)
2 bunches of watercress, washed, trimmed and dried
150 ml (5 fl oz/⅔ cup) Homemade Mayonnaise (see page 101)

1 To make the Watercress Mayonnaise, purée the watercress in a food processor or blender until finely ground. Add the mayonnaise and blend again.
2 Place the prawns (shrimp) flat in a shallow dish. Mix the lime juice with the garlic and olive oil and add plenty of pepper. Spoon this over the prawns and leave for 2–3 hours, covered with cling film (plastic wrap).
3 Toss the prawns in the marinade and leave, covered, for a further hour.
4 Oil a long-handled, hinged wire basket, put the prawns in it, and place on top of the grill. Alternatively, thread the prawns on to the skewers, and place directly on the grill. Barbecue lightly on both sides.
5 Serve with the Watercress Mayonnaise, or with lime wedges.
Illustrated on pages 88–9

June is the month of sounds. They melt and merge
Softer than shallow waves in pebbled surge
Forward and backward in a summer cove;
The very music of the month is warm,
The very music sings the song of love.
Vita Sackville-West: "The Garden"

SALADS & SIDE DISHES

CHINESE CARROT SALAD

This simple yet sublime salad lends itself really well not only to barbecues but also to picnics—it improves on keeping and is not really affected by the temperature at which it is kept. The black bean sauce is available in jars from Chinese delicatessens.

SERVES 4

6 large carrots, peeled and finely grated
60 ml (4 tbsp) chopped mixed fresh herbs, such as parsley, chives, coriander
red cabbage or radicchio leaf, to serve (optional)
FOR THE BLACK BEAN DRESSING
22.5 ml (1½ tbsp) black bean sauce
15 ml (1 tbsp) grated fresh ginger root
30 ml (2 tbsp) raspberry vinegar
15 ml (1 tbsp) soy sauce
75 ml (5 tbsp) dark sesame oil

1 Mix the grated carrots with the herbs in a bowl, or heap the mixture in a red cabbage or radicchio leaf.
2 Stir all the dressing ingredients together until well blended. Leave to stand for 10 minutes before using.
3 Coat the carrot salad with the dressing.

FLAGEOLETS AL PESTO

This makes a lovely salad for an alfresco meal, be it a barbecue in the garden or a picnic in the countryside. Decorate the salad with chive flowers if they are available—the mauve flowers contrast beautifully with the green pesto. (Pesto is an Italian sauce made from puréed basil, garlic, olive oil and pine nuts; it is available from delicatessens and some supermarkets.)

SERVES 2–3

400 g (14 oz) canned flageolets or navy beans, drained
45 ml (3 tbsp) pesto
60 ml (4 tbsp) Vinaigrette (see page 42)
shredded lettuce
chive flowers, to garnish (optional)

1 Put the flageolets or navy beans into a bowl.
2 Mix the pesto with half of the Vinaigrette, blending them thoroughly.
3 Dress the lettuce with the rest of the Vinaigrette and put into a serving dish. Pile the flageolets on top, and garnish with chive flowers if available.

CHEESY TOMATOES

Like Flageolets al Pesto (see this page), this dish derives its exquisite flavour from the Italian sauce pesto, which is used here with cheese and rice as a filling for the tomatoes. As the cheese melts in the heat of the barbecue, it blends delectably with the pesto and rice. (Basmati rice, which comes from India, is narrower and more pointed than other long-grain rice and cooks more quickly. It is available from delicatessens and some supermarkets.)

SERVES 6

6 large tomatoes
salt and pepper
225 g (8 oz/1 cup) semi-soft cheese, such as Bel Paese, diced small
225 g (8 oz/1½ cups) cooked basmati rice
30 ml (2 tbsp) pesto
small bunch of fresh basil, chopped

1 Cut a lid off the top of the tomatoes and scoop out the insides to leave them hollow. Sprinkle the shells with a little salt and turn upside down to drain.
2 Mix the diced cheese, cooked rice, pesto and chopped basil together to form the stuffing. Add salt and pepper to taste.
3 Wipe the insides of the tomatoes dry and fill them with the stuffing. Wrap them in foil. Barbecue the tomatoes on the grill for about 15–20 minutes until the tomatoes are tender and the cheese melts.

MARINATED MUSHROOM KEBABS

Mushrooms steeped in an aromatic marinade make excellent kebabs for a barbecue. One of the nicest ways of eating them is inside warm pitta bread.

SERVES 4

450 g (1 lb/4 cups) button mushrooms
4 pitta breads
mayonnaise
shredded crisp lettuce
Vinaigrette (see page 42)

FOR THE MARINADE

100 ml (4 fl oz/½ cup) white wine
30 ml (2 tbsp) chopped fresh herbs, such as parsley, lovage, tarragon, fennel
75 ml (5 tbsp) olive oil
2 large garlic cloves, skinned and crushed

1 Mix all the marinade ingredients together in a large bowl. Leave to stand for at least 30 minutes.

2 Marinate the mushrooms in the white wine marinade for several hours.

3 Skewer the mushrooms on to kebab sticks and barbecue on the grill for about 15 minutes until cooked through, brushing with the marinade as they cook.

4 Meanwhile, wrap the pitta breads in foil, and warm them on the barbecue grill for about 10–15 minutes. Unwrap the pitta breads, split them open and spread the insides with mayonnaise. Dress the shredded lettuce with Vinaigrette, and put a little on the bottom of the bread.

5 Remove the mushrooms from the sticks and put them on the shredded lettuce. Close the pitta bread and serve.

OVERLEAF (from left to right): Flageolets al Pesto *(page 96)*, Chinese Carrot Salad *(page 96)*

TOMATOES WITH BLUE CHEESE AND YOGURT DRESSING

The summery taste of tomatoes in high season is enhanced by this distinctive dressing of blue cheese, yogurt and tarragon vinegar. Simplicity itself, the salad is garnished with chopped chives.

SERVES 4–6

700 g (1½ lb) ripe tomatoes
small bunch of chives, finely chopped
FOR THE BLUE CHEESE AND YOGURT DRESSING
75 ml (5 tbsp) plain yogurt
25 g (1 oz/¼ cup) blue cheese, crumbled
10 ml (2 tsp) tarragon vinegar

1 To make the dressing, blend the yogurt with the cheese until smooth. Stir in the vinegar.
2 Pour boiling water over the tomatoes and leave for 1 minute. Peel off the skins and slice the tomatoes thinly.
3 Toss the tomatoes in the dressing until they are well coated. Put into a dish and sprinkle with the chives.

MIXED SALAD WITH TAHINI MAYONNAISE

Here, a succulent salad of lightly cooked summer vegetables is mixed with crisp shredded Chinese cabbage. Tossed in a mayonnaise which is blended with tahini (sesame paste), it makes a delectable salad to go with a barbecued meal.

SERVES 6

1 yellow pepper, quartered
225 g (8 oz) cooked and sliced courgettes (zucchini)
225 g (8 oz) French (green) beans, cut into 1 cm
(½ inch) slices
225 g (8 oz) tomatoes, cut into wedges
400 g (14 oz) can sweetcorn (corn) kernels, drained
½ Chinese cabbage, shredded
FOR THE TAHINI MAYONNAISE
10 ml (2 tsp) tahini (see page 9)
10 ml (2 tsp) plain yogurt
10 ml (2 tsp) dark sesame oil (see page 10)
40 ml (8 tsp) Homemade Mayonnaise (see page 101)

1 To make the Tahini Mayonnaise, blend the tahini (sesame paste) with the yogurt until smooth, then stir in the dark sesame oil. Stir into the Homemade Mayonnaise and mix thoroughly.

2 Grill (broil) the pepper for 5–10 minutes, skin side up. Peel off the skin, remove seeds and cut into slices.

3 Mix the salad ingredients in a large salad bowl. Just before serving, dress the salad with the Tahini Mayonnaise, and toss thoroughly.

HOMEMADE MAYONNAISE

A homemade mayonnaise makes all the difference to summer salads. This version is less likely to curdle because it contains only one egg, and the use of the egg white as well as the yolk helps to make it thick.

MAKES ABOUT 320 ml ($\frac{1}{2}$ pint/$1\frac{1}{4}$ cups)

1 egg
5 ml (1 tsp) dry mustard
salt and pepper
300 ml ($\frac{1}{2}$ pint/$1\frac{1}{4}$ cups) sunflower oil
about 15 ml (1 tbsp) lemon juice

1 Put the egg into a food processor or blender and add the mustard, salt and pepper.

2 With the machine working, slowly pour in a thin stream of oil, pausing from time to time to allow the mayonnaise to thicken. Be careful not to pour too fast at the beginning or the mixture could curdle.

3 Thin with the lemon juice to taste at the end. Store in a screw-top jar in the refrigerator for up to 1 week.

BUTTERY MUSHROOMS WITH CORIANDER

Flat mushrooms are spread with butter and cheese mixed with garlic and coriander, then barbecued.

SERVES 4

50 g (2 oz/$\frac{1}{4}$ cup) low-fat soft cheese such as Quark or fromage frais

50 g (2 oz/$\frac{1}{4}$ cup) butter
1 garlic clove, skinned and crushed
10 ml (2 tsp) grated lime rind
bunch of fresh coriander, chopped
salt and pepper
450 g (1 lb/4 cups) large, flat mushrooms, stalks removed

1 Cream the butter with the cheese in a bowl. Beat in the garlic, lime rind and coriander. Add salt and pepper to taste.

2 Spread the inside of each mushroom with the mixture. Put on to a barbecue plate or small roasting tin (pan), and cover with foil. Barbecue for about 20 minutes until the mushrooms are soft.

TOSSED SALAD WITH SESAME SEED MAYONNAISE

A great salad bowl full of lettuce, watercress, herbs and fennel looks beautiful with a dash of red radicchio among all the greens. The Sesame Seed Mayonnaise is a soft dressing with an irresistible texture, ideal for a special occasion barbecue.

SERVES 8

2 crisp lettuces, trimmed
2 bunches of watercress, trimmed
1 small head of radicchio, trimmed
large bunch of fresh herbs, such as lovage, tarragon, chives, marjoram
1 fennel bulb, sliced
FOR THE SESAME SEED MAYONNAISE
15 ml (1 tbsp) sesame seeds
75 ml (5 tbsp) Homemade Mayonnaise (see this page)
1 garlic clove, skinned and crushed

1 To make the Sesame Seed Mayonnaise, brown the sesame seeds under a medium grill (broiler), shaking the tray so that they brown evenly all over. Cool. Stir the sesame seeds into the Homemade Mayonnaise with the garlic. Leave to stand for at least 30 minutes.

2 Put the greens, herbs and fennel into a salad bowl, and mix. Dress with the Sesame Seed Mayonnaise, tossing thoroughly.

GARLICKY CORN ON THE COB

This garlicky corn on the cob is heavenly with Hot Basil Bread (see page 133) that has been wrapped in foil and barbecued on the grill for about 10 minutes.

SERVES 6

6 ears of corn, husks removed and cut in half crosswise
5 ml (1 tsp) grated lemon rind
30 ml (2 tbsp) soy sauce
60 ml (4 tbsp) olive oil
1 garlic clove, skinned and crushed
pepper

1 Put all the ingredients in a bowl. Cover with cling film (plastic wrap) and marinate overnight.
2 Lift out the corn, and wrap individually in foil, twisting the ends for a tight seal. Barbecue for about 15–20 minutes in the coals or about 30–40 minutes on the barbecue grill, turning several times.
Illustrated on page 93

LEEKS IN BLUE-CHEESE DRESSING

A delicious salad for a barbecue—or simply when dining in a conservatory or sunporch on one of those fine days that aren't quite as warm as they look. It is rich, with strong flavours, and can be served on its own, as an hors d'oeuvre or as a side salad.

SERVES 4

20 small, tender leeks, trimmed and washed
75 g (3 oz/¾ cup) walnuts, finely chopped
45 ml (3 tbsp) finely chopped fresh parsley
FOR THE BLUE-CHEESE DRESSING
75 g (3 oz/¾ cup) mild blue cheese, crumbled
150 ml (¼ pint/⅔ cup) Vinaigrette (see page 42)

1 Cook the leeks in boiling salted water for 10–12 minutes until they are tender, but still hold their shape. Cool. Arrange in a shallow serving dish. Sprinkle with the walnuts and parsley.
2 To make the dressing, stir the cheese into the Vinaigrette and blend. Spoon over the leeks and serve.

DESSERTS

MELT-IN-THE-MOUTH BANANAS

These bananas can be prepared in advance, then barbecued as people are finishing the main course.

SERVES 6

6 bananas, peeled
45 ml (3 tbsp) lemon juice
90 ml (6 tbsp) Cointreau or other orange liqueur
40 g (1½ oz/3 tbsp) soft light brown sugar
2.5 ml (½ tsp) ground cinnamon
50 g (2 oz/¼ cup) unsalted butter

1 Put each banana on to a piece of foil and gather the foil around the fruit. Mix the lemon juice, Cointreau, sugar and cinnamon together, then pour some over each banana. Dot with the butter. Seal the foil tightly.
2 Barbecue on the coals for about 5–10 minutes, or on the grill for about 10–15 minutes, turning once, until the bananas are soft and the liquid has caramelized.

I was rich in flowers and trees,
Humming-birds and honey-bees;
For my sport the squirrel played,
Plied the snouted mole his spade;
For my taste the blackberry cone
Purpled over hedge and stone;
Laughed the brook for my delight
Through the day and through the night,
Whispering at the garden wall,
Talked with me from fall to fall;
Mine the sand-rimmed pickerel pond,
Mine the walnut slopes beyond,
Mine, on bending orchard trees,
Apples of Hesperides!
John Greenleaf Whittier: "The Barefoot Boy"

FRUIT SALAD ON A STICK

Hot fruit salad with a difference! These fruit kebabs round off a barbecue party very elegantly.

SERVES 6

50 g (2 oz/¼ cup) butter
45 ml (3 tbsp) golden (light corn) syrup
1.4 kg (3 lb) fresh fruit, such as cubed melon, large strawberries, cubed fresh pineapple, cubed apples, cubed pears, seedless grapes
crème fraîche (see page 10), to serve

1 Warm the butter and syrup together in a small pan until the butter has melted.
2 Thread the fruit on to skewers.
3 Barbecue the fruit on the grill over the embers, for about 5 minutes, brushing with the butter and syrup mixture as you turn them to cook all over. Serve the barbecued kebabs with crème fraîche.

BARBECUED PEARS

The flavour and texture of pears cooked in this way have to be experienced to be believed!

SERVES 6

6 ripe pears, peeled, cored and cut into half
TO SERVE
crème fraîche (see page 10)
fresh orange juice
grated orange rind
icing (confectioners') sugar

1 Wrap each pear in a foil parcel with 15 ml (1 tbsp) water. Seal tightly.
2 Barbecue on the grill for about 40 minutes until the fruit is soft. Serve with crème fraîche, flavoured with a little fresh orange juice, grated orange rind, and icing (confectioners') sugar to taste.

CHAPTER SEVEN

Light Suppers

On a cool summer's evening, it is pure pleasure to eat supper on the patio or lawn around a table laid informally for a light meal. Long, hot days demand light food, with plenty of salads; simple fish dishes and lightly cooked summer vegetables are the order of the day. Choose meals that are quick to prepare and are easily transferred from kitchen to garden, so that you too can relax and enjoy the calm of the evening.

MENU SUGGESTIONS

MENU 32
Ruchetta ai Funghi page 116
Tuna Steaks with Fennel page 110
new potatoes; French (green) beans
Tomato Salad with Tarragon page 119
Black Currant Shortcake page 122

•

MENU 33
Chinese Ratatouille page 110
new potatoes; mangetout (snow peas)
Salade Noisette page 118
Simple Mango Sorbet page 122

•

MENU 34
Omelette Primavera page 114
buttered fresh spinach
Jumbo Caesar Salad page 118
Golden Pear Tart page 125

•

MENU 35
Oriental Steamed Bass page 112
Rice Noodles with Summer Vegetables page 116
Hot Radicchio Italian Style page 119
Crunchy Apricot Layer page 122

MAIN DISHES

CHINESE RATATOUILLE

Flavoured with basil and five-spice powder (a sharp, fragrant mixture of five spices—star anise, Chinese pepper, cloves, cinnamon and fennel seeds—which is available from Chinese delicatessens) and sprinkled with fresh coriander leaves, this oriental version of ratatouille makes a delightful summer meal. As it can be served hot or cold, it is also excellent for a picnic, with chapatis (flat, unleavened bread from India), and a crisp salad kept fresh in the cool-box (ice chest).

SERVES 4

30 ml (2 tbsp) butter
15 ml (1 tbsp) olive oil
2 large garlic cloves, skinned and finely chopped
225 g (8 oz/2 cups) aubergine (eggplant), cubed
225 g (8 oz/2 cups) courgettes (zucchini), cubed
1 large cucumber, peeled and cubed
100 g (4 oz/⅔ cup) baby carrots, sliced
100 g (4 oz/1 cup) waterchestnuts, sliced
30 ml (2 tbsp) chopped chives
small bunch of basil leaves
225 g (8 oz/1 cup) canned tomatoes, drained and chopped, the liquid reserved
10 ml (2 tsp) five-spice powder
salt and pepper
TO GARNISH
chopped fresh coriander
nasturtium flowers (optional)

1 Heat the butter and oil in a large pan and cook the garlic for 1–2 minutes.
2 Add the aubergine (eggplant), courgettes (zucchini), cucumber and carrots. Cook over a medium heat for 2 minutes further, then add the waterchestnuts, chives, basil and canned tomatoes with their juices.
3 Stir in the five-spice powder and simmer for 5 minutes or until all the vegetables are just firm. Add salt and pepper to taste.
4 Sprinkle the ratatouille with the chopped coriander, and the flowers if available. Serve hot, warm or cold.

TUNA STEAKS WITH FENNEL

This dish of fresh tuna steaks with a fennel, garlic and basil sauce is especially good with buttered new potatoes and French (green) beans, or with a salad such as Salade Noisette (see page 118).

SERVES 6

2 fennel bulbs, chopped
200 ml (7 fl oz/⅞ cup) olive oil
5 garlic cloves, skinned and finely chopped
salt and pepper
a few basil sprigs
2 large tuna steaks, 2 cm (¾ inch) thick

1 Place the fennel in a saucepan with one-quarter of the olive oil, 2 of the chopped garlic cloves and salt and pepper. Simmer gently for 5 minutes.
2 Blend the basil with the remaining garlic and olive oil in a food processor or blender. Add salt and pepper to taste, then add to the fennel mixture.
3 Fry the tuna steaks in a non-stick pan using very little olive oil. Add them to the pan containing the fennel, cover and steam for 1 minute—do not overcook the tuna or it will dry out.
4 Divide each steak into 3 pieces and serve with the fennel, basil and garlic sauce.

ORIENTAL STEAMED BASS

A whole fish, steamed with black bean and garlic sauce (available in jars from Chinese delicatessens) and ginger, is epicurean food for a summer's evening.

SERVES 4

1 whole bass, weighing about 1 kg (2–2½ lb), head removed if preferred
5 cm (2 inch) piece fresh ginger root, peeled and finely grated
6 spring onions (scallions), trimmed and finely sliced
30 ml (2 tbsp) black bean and garlic sauce
30 ml (2 tbsp) soy sauce
30 ml (2 tbsp) dark sesame oil
30 ml (2 tbsp) sunflower oil
fresh coriander leaves, to garnish (optional)
fresh ginger root, to garnish (optional)

1 Slash the sides of the bass. Make a paste with the ginger, all but a few of the spring onions (scallions), the black bean and garlic sauce and soy sauce. Rub into the incisions.
2 Steam the fish in an oval steamer or a fish kettle (fish poacher) for 10–12 minutes or until cooked through to the centre. Put on to a warm serving dish, reserving the juices.
3 Heat the sesame and sunflower oils together and, when very hot, pour over the fish to crisp the skin. Pour the cooking juices around the dish and garnish with the remaining spring onion slices and either coriander leaves or ginger root, peeled, sliced and then cut into long, thin strips.

I sing of Brooks, of Blossoms, Birds and Bowers:
Of April, May, of June, and July-Flowers.
Robert Herrick: "The Argument of his Book"

RIGHT: *Oriental Steamed Bass (this page)*

OMELETTE PRIMAVERA

So often the outrageously simple is superlatively delicious. With really fresh ingredients this omelette is fantastic for an informal alfresco supper. Serve it with warm bread and salad.

SERVES 2

175 g (6 oz) new potatoes, scrubbed
1 mint sprig
40 g (1½ oz/3 tbsp) butter
small bunch of chives, finely chopped
4 eggs
60 ml (4 tbsp) double (heavy) cream
salt and pepper
olive oil, for cooking
25 g (1 oz/¼ cup) Cheddar cheese, finely grated

1 Cook the new potatoes in boiling water with a sprig of mint for about 15 minutes until cooked through but still waxy and slightly crisp. Discard the mint.
2 Drain the potatoes, cool them a little, then slice them. Toss in the butter with the chives.
3 Beat the eggs, add the cream and beat again. Add salt and pepper to taste.
4 Heat a little olive oil in a large, heavy shallow pan and pour in the egg mixture. As it begins to set, draw it in from the sides of the pan. Turn the heat down to set the omelette gently, so it does not cook too fast.
5 Lay the cooked potatoes on to one half of the omelette, and fold the other half over. Transfer the omelette to a warm serving dish. Sprinkle with finely grated cheese and serve at once.

A Book of Verses underneath the Bough,
A Jug of Wine, a Loaf of Bread—and Thou
Beside me singing in the Wilderness—
Oh, Wilderness were Paradise enow!
Edward Fitzgerald: "The Rubaiyat of Omar Khayyam"

SALADS & SIDE DISHES

RUCHETTA AI FUNGHI

I first tasted this dish in Umbria, in central Italy, where sweet rocket (arugula) is used as the herb. Pecorino is a hard Italian cheese made from matured sheep's milk; if you can't find it, use fresh Parmesan cheese instead. Although hard cheese like Pecorino or Parmesan is more often eaten after being melted, here it is served unheated, which allows its flavour to be enjoyed to the full.

SERVES 4

12 large button mushrooms, trimmed and very finely sliced
90 ml (6 tbsp) coarsely chopped mixed fresh herbs, such as sweet rocket (arugula), sorrel, lovage, marjoram, fennel, lemon balm, parsley
olive oil
175 g (6 oz) Pecorino or Parmesan cheese, finely slivered
nasturtium flowers, to garnish (optional)

1 On a large, shallow platter, layer mushrooms and herbs, dribbling olive oil over each layer.
2 Cover the mushrooms and herbs with the cheese. Garnish with nasturtium flowers if available.

RICE NOODLES WITH SUMMER VEGETABLES

Rice noodles are excellent fare for summer, being very light and digestible. This stir-fry of fresh broccoli, baby carrots and asparagus or mangetout (snow peas) combines beautifully with the noodles for an informal, easy alfresco supper.

SERVES 3–4

225 g (8 oz) rice noodles
225 g (8 oz) broccoli
225 g (8 oz) baby carrots
225 g (8 oz) asparagus or mangetout (snow peas), trimmed
30 ml (2 tbsp) olive oil
2 garlic cloves, skinned and finely sliced
5–6 spring onions (scallions), trimmed and finely sliced
2.5 cm (1 inch) piece fresh ginger root, peeled and grated
30–45 ml (2–3 tbsp) soy sauce, to taste
30 ml (2 tbsp) dark sesame oil

1 Soak the noodles in warm water for 20 minutes. Drain the noodles, then dry them thoroughly on a clean cloth.
2 Steam the broccoli and carrots for 3 minutes, and the asparagus or mangetout (snow peas) for 2 minutes. Cut the vegetables into small pieces.
3 Heat the olive oil in a large pan or wok and gently stir fry the garlic, spring onions (scallions) and ginger. Increase the heat a little and add the vegetables. Toss until well coated and heated through.
4 Add the soy sauce and dark sesame oil and toss again. Toss in the rice noodles and mix thoroughly, stirring briskly.
5 Transfer to a warm serving platter and serve at once.

RIGHT: *Ruchetta ai Funghi (this page)*

SALADE NOISETTE

This salad features a variety of contrasting textures: delicate oak leaf (leaf) lettuce with its lovely bronze colour and its large, curled and fringed leaves, crisp radicchio, soft mushrooms and crunchy hazelnuts, tossed in a lemony yogurt dressing sweetened with honey. In late spring it can be garnished with a spray of white hawthorn.

SERVES 4

1 oak leaf (leaf) lettuce, trimmed
6 radicchio leaves, torn
small bunch of fresh marjoram leaves
6 medium button mushrooms, finely sliced
50 g (2 oz/½ cup) hazelnuts, halved and toasted
hawthorn flowers, to garnish (optional)
FOR THE LEMONY YOGURT DRESSING
30 ml (2 tbsp) olive oil
juice of ½ lemon
10 ml (2 tsp) clear honey
75 g (3 oz/scant ½ cup) plain yogurt

ABOVE: Hot Radicchio Italian Style (page 119)

1 Put all the salad ingredients into a salad bowl.
2 Blend the dressing ingredients together. Toss the salad in the dressing just before serving. Garnish with hawthorn flowers if available.

JUMBO CAESAR SALAD

This is one of my favourites of all the supper salads to eat alfresco, because it incorporates the freshness and real flavour of a seasonal salad. Crisp, nutty lettuce with freshly grated Parmesan cheese, the crunch of croûtons plus a garlicky dressing, add up to a feast for a late meal in the garden.

SERVES 2

4 slices of day-old bread
vegetable oil for frying
1 large crisp lettuce, such as cos (romaine)

50 g (2 oz/½ cup) fresh Parmesan cheese, finely grated
sea salt
FOR THE GARLIC VINAIGRETTE
Vinaigrette (see page 42)
garlic cloves, skinned and crushed

1 To make croûtons, cut the crusts off the bread. Cut the bread into tiny cubes and fry in oil, turning frequently so that they brown evenly all over. When golden and crisp, drain throughly on paper towels.
2 To make the Garlic Vinaigrette, add garlic to taste to the basic Vinaigrette. Leave to stand for at least 30 minutes before using.
3 Cut or tear the lettuce into manageable pieces. Toss the lettuce in the Garlic Vinaigrette and arrange in a large salad bowl. Sprinkle the Parmesan cheese and sea salt over the top and toss the salad to thoroughly mix.
4 Just before serving, sprinkle the croûtons over the top, toss them lightly into the salad and serve.

TOMATO SALAD WITH TARRAGON

The flavours of this salad are perfect for a summer dinner: refreshing and light, with a slightly spicy zest. It also makes delectable picnic fare.

SERVES 4

700 g (1½ lb) tomatoes
10 ml (2 tsp) chopped fresh tarragon
10 ml (2 tsp) chopped chives
tarragon leaves, to garnish
FOR THE SESAME OIL DRESSING
60 ml (4 tbsp) Vinaigrette (see page 42)
30 ml (2 tbsp) dark sesame oil
5 ml (1 tsp) soy sauce

1 Pour boiling water over the tomatoes and leave for 1 minute. Peel off the skins and cut the flesh into cubes. Drain in a colander for 20–30 minutes.
2 Mix the Vinaigrette with the sesame oil and soy sauce.
3 Just before serving, combine the tomatoes with the chopped tarragon and chives in a salad bowl. Toss the tomatoes in the dressing. Scatter tarragon leaves over the salad for a garnish.
Illustrated on pages 50–1

To one who has been long in city pent,
'T is very sweet to look into the fair
And open face of heaven,—to breathe a prayer
Full in the smile of the blue firmament.
Who is more happy, when, with heart's content,
Fatigued he sinks into some pleasant lair
Of wavy grass, and reads a debonair
and gentle tale of love and languishment?
John Keats: "To One Who Has Been Long in City Pent"

HOT RADICCHIO ITALIAN STYLE

This salad can be served as a side dish, as an hors d'oeuvre, or even as a main course with various salad accompaniments. Well suited to alfresco meals, this is basically an Italian dish. Dolcelatte is a delicate form of Gorgonzola, a type of Italian blue cheese. Radicchio, or red chicory, was also developed in Italy; and balsamic vinegar is a fine Italian wine vinegar.

SERVES 4

2 heads of radicchio, trimmed
50 g (2 oz/¼ cup) butter
175 g (6 oz/1½ cups) Dolcelatte cheese, finely diced
30 ml (2 tbsp) balsamic vinegar
15 ml (1 tbsp) chopped chives
salt and pepper

1 Cut each radicchio head in half lengthwise. Melt three-quarters of the butter in a large, shallow pan and add the radicchio, cut side down. Cook over a moderate heat for 4–5 minutes, turning each one over to cook the uncut side too, until the leaves have wilted.
2 Sprinkle the Dolcelatte over the cut side of each radicchio half, and place under a very hot grill (broiler) until it melts. Transfer to 4 warm plates.
3 Add the vinegar to the pan with the remaining butter and the chives. Shake the pan until the butter has melted, then cook over a medium heat for 1 minute.
4 Spoon the mixture over the radicchio and add salt and pepper to taste. Serve immediately.

DESSERTS

SIMPLE MANGO SORBET

To me, mango is the most epicurean of all fruits. This simple sorbet, which is so easy to make, is a useful standby through the summer months, and is a perfect way to round off an alfresco supper.

SERVES 4–6

100 g (4 oz/½ cup) granulated sugar
150 ml (¼ pint/⅔ cup) water
1 large ripe mango, peeled and stoned (pitted)

1 Put the sugar and water into a saucepan and bring to the boil, stirring. Boil for 2 minutes. Set aside to cool a little while you prepare the mango.
2 Purée the mango flesh in a food processor or blender.
3 Mix the purée with the cooled syrup and beat well. Put the mixture into a freezer container and freeze for at least 4 hours.
4 Allow to stand at room temperature for at least 30 minutes before serving.

BLACK CURRANT SHORTCAKE

Tasting of summer, this dessert is a superb finishing touch to an alfresco supper. The light shortcake topping is simply delectable.

SERVES 3–4

350 g (12 oz/3 cups) fresh black currants, stalks removed
30 ml (2 tbsp) caster (superfine) sugar
100 g (4 oz/1 cup) plain (all-purpose) flour
2.5 ml (½ tsp) baking powder
40 g (1½ oz/3 tbsp) butter
75 g (3 oz/⅓ cup) soft light brown sugar
vanilla ice cream, to serve

1 Arrange the black currants over the bottom of a 20.5 cm (8 inch) sandwich tin (round layer cake pan) and sprinkle the caster (superfine) sugar over the top.
2 Sift the flour with the baking powder into a bowl and rub in the butter until the mixture is crumbly. Stir in the brown sugar. Spread the mixture over the fruit, pressing it down lightly with a fork.
3 Bake at 180°C/350°F/mark 4 for 25–30 minutes until the topping is a pale golden. Serve with vanilla ice cream.

CRUNCHY APRICOT LAYER

A delightful concoction of a crunchy, nutty base, covered with thick Greek yogurt, topped with sliced fresh apricots and decorated with strawberries.

SERVES 4

700 g (1½ lb) fresh ripe apricots, stoned (pitted) and quartered
granulated sugar, to taste
75 g (3 oz/6 tbsp) margarine, diced
100 g (4 oz/1⅓ cups) medium whole-grain oats
50 g (2 oz/½ cup) wholemeal (wholewheat) flour
75 g (3 oz/6 tbsp) demerara (light brown) sugar
40 g (1½ oz/scant ½ cup) nibbed (coarsely chopped) almonds
225 g (8 oz/1 cup) Greek yogurt (see page 9)
strawberries, halved, to decorate

1 Grease a Swiss roll tin (jelly roll pan).
2 Put the prepared apricots into a dish and sprinkle with sugar to taste. Toss.
3 Rub the margarine into the oats and flour in a bowl until thoroughly mixed. Stir in the sugar and the almonds. Press the mixture into the prepared tin.
4 Bake at 190°C/375°F/mark 5 for 15–20 minutes until golden. Cool completely, then break it up into pieces.
5 Cover the base of a shallow dessert dish with the crunchy oat mixture and coat with the Greek yogurt. Arrange the apricots over the top. Decorate with the strawberries and serve chilled.

GOLDEN PEAR TART

This classic pear tart is baked with a ground almond topping until golden-brown.

SERVES 6–8

FOR THE PASTRY
75 g (3 oz/6 tbsp) caster (superfine) sugar
150 g (5 oz/½ cup plus 2 tbsp) butter or margarine
225 g (8 oz/2 cups) plain (all-purpose) flour, sifted

FOR THE FILLING
100 g (4 oz/½ cup) butter
100 g (4 oz/½ cup) granulated sugar
2 eggs
25 g (1 oz/¼ cup) plain (all-purpose) flour
150 g (5 oz/1¼ cups) ground almonds
5 ml (1 tsp) vanilla extract
4 ripe firm pears, peeled, cored and sliced
30 ml (2 tbsp) apricot jam, warmed

1 To make the pastry, melt the butter and stir the sugar into it over a gentle heat until dissolved. Stir in the sifted flour and work to a smooth dough. Chill.
2 Press the pastry into a 25 cm (10 inch) flan tin (pie pan), prick the base with a fork and cover with foil. Weight down the pastry with dried beans.
3 Bake at 170°C/325°F/mark 3 for 15 minutes. Remove the beans and foil.
4 Beat the butter, sugar, eggs, flour, ground almonds and vanilla together. Spread this over the pastry. Arrange the sliced pears decoratively over the top and brush with the warmed apricot jam.
5 Bake at 220°C/425°F/mark 7 for 15–20 minutes until set and golden-brown. Serve at room temperature.

The day is done, and the darkness
Falls from the wings of Night,
As a feather is wafted downward
From an eagle in his flight.
Henry Wadsworth Longfellow: "The Day is Done"

LEFT: *Golden Pear Tart (this page)*

CHAPTER EIGHT

Dinner at Dusk

Nothing is more idyllic than a candlelit dinner alfresco, as the diminishing light fades into dusk. The food should be light but elegant, and a summery soup or exotic salad makes a good first course. For the main course, poultry or fish served with an interesting sauce is ideal, accompanied by a chilled white wine. Vegetables of the season and perhaps a salad to follow, then a light fruit dessert, bring a lovely summer's evening to a close.

LEFT (from left to right): Spicy Summer Vegetable Salad *(page 138),* Pasta Salad with Basil and Cheese *(page 45)*

MENU SUGGESTIONS

MENU 36
Asparagus Soup with Coriander page 133
Salmon with Sorrel page 134
new potatoes; mangetout (snow peas)
Spicy Summer Vegetable Salad page 138
Elderflower Ice Cream page 140

•

MENU 37
Mangetout (Snow Peas) and Avocado Vinaigrette page 133, *served with*
Hot Basil Bread page 133
Monkfish in Lettuce Parcels page 134
buttered rice; baby carrots
Chilled Melon Dessert page 140

•

MENU 38
Smoked Salmon Rolls page 130, *served with walnut bread*
Seafood Stir-fry with Saffron Noodles page 136
Green Salad with Chinese Dressing page 139
Flaming Peaches page 140

•

MENU 39
Hot Radicchio Italian Style page 119
Cheesy Chicken in Filo Pastry page 135
Noodles with Spicy Peanut Butter Dressing page 138
Gingery Tomatoes page 139
Raspberry Almond Crunch page 142

FIRST COURSES

SMOKED SALMON ROLLS

These little smoked salmon rolls served on paper-thin slices of walnut bread are an excellent party dish.

MAKES 15

15 slices of smoked salmon
15 paper-thin slices of walnut bread (optional)
butter, for spreading
soft lettuce leaves
FOR THE FILLING
175 g (6 oz/¾ cup) full-fat soft cheese (cream cheese)
2.5 ml (½ tsp) each grated orange and lemon rind
10 ml (2 tsp) green peppercorns, drained and crushed
30 ml (2 tbsp) chopped fresh chives
10 ml (2 tsp) chopped fresh thyme
TO GARNISH
bunch of chives, blanched
tomato wedges

1 Mash all the filling ingredients together and chill.
2 Put a heaped teaspoon of filling on to the middle of each salmon slice and roll up into little parcels, tucking in the ends. Tie the parcels with the chives. Chill.
3 If serving with walnut bread, butter the bread and remove the crusts. Cover each slice with a lettuce leaf then a salmon roll. Garnish with tomato wedges.

So the good gardener will sow his drift
Of larkspur and forget-me-not
To fill black space, or recklessly to pick;
And gay nasturtium writing up a fence
Splotching with mock of sunlight sunless days
When latening summer brings the usual mist.
Vita Sackville-West: "The Garden"

RIGHT: *Smoked Salmon Rolls (this page)*

MANGETOUT (SNOW PEA) AND AVOCADO VINAIGRETTE

An elegant arrangement of mangetout (snow peas), asparagus, avocado and pine nuts set on lettuce, makes a beautiful beginning to a dinner party alfresco. Serve it with Hot Basil Bread (see this page).

SERVES 6

350 g (12 oz) asparagus, trimmed
700 g (1½ lb) mangetout (snow peas), trimmed
2 ripe avocados, peeled and stoned (pitted)
50 g (2 oz/½ cup) pine nuts, browned
75 ml (5 tbsp) Garlic Vinaigrette (see page 119)
soft lettuce leaves, to garnish

1 Steam the asparagus for 3–4 minutes until cooked but still crisp. Cool.
2 Steam the mangetout (snow peas) for 2–3 minutes until cooked but still slightly crisp. Cool.
3 Cut the avocado flesh into pieces—the flesh must be ripe but not over-ripe, so that it holds its shape.
4 Combine the mangetout, avocado and pine nuts, and toss in the Garlic Vinaigrette.
5 Line a serving dish with soft lettuce leaves, then pile the mixture into it. Arrange the asparagus over the top of the mangetout and avocado.

LEFT: *Mangetout (Snow Pea) and Avocado Vinaigrette (this page)*

HOT BASIL BREAD

This aromatic bread is one of the highlights of summer. Serve it with Mangetout (Snow Pea) and Avocado Vinaigrette (see this page) as a first course.

SERVES 3–4

small bunch of basil, finely chopped
100 g (4 oz/½ cup) butter, melted
1 long French baguette

1 Mix the basil into the melted butter. Alternatively, you can mince the basil in a food processor or blender, then add the melted butter and blend again. Chill.
2 Cut the French bread into slices, not quite cutting through the bottom. Spread both sides of all the slices with the basil butter. Wrap tightly in foil.
3 Bake at 180°C/350°F mark 4 for 15 minutes, loosening the foil for the last few minutes. Serve hot.
Illustrated on page 93

ASPARAGUS SOUP WITH CORIANDER

A table set on the terrace, candles lit for dinner at dusk: this summery green soup gets the evening off to a great start. It is also good cold for picnics.

SERVES 6

900 g (2 lb) asparagus, cut into 5 cm (2 inch) pieces
1.4 litres (2½ pints/1½ quarts) vegetable stock (broth)
3 spring onions (scallions), trimmed and chopped
175 g (6 oz/¾ cup) crème fraîche (see page 10)
60 ml (4 tbsp) chopped fresh coriander
salt and pepper
coriander leaves, to garnish

1 Simmer the asparagus pieces in the stock for 8–10 minutes until very tender. Cool slightly.
2 Purée the asparagus in a food processor or blender with some of the stock (broth). Pour into a large saucepan. Stir over a very low heat, adding the rest of the stock, the spring onions (scallions), crème fraîche and coriander. Add salt and pepper to taste. Cook for 3–4 minutes, then garnish with coriander leaves. Serve.
Illustrated on page 129

MAIN DISHES

SALMON WITH SORREL

A simple but classic dish of lightly sautéed salmon fillets, coated with a summery sauce of sorrel, crème fraîche and white wine.

SERVES 6

200 ml (7 fl oz/$\frac{7}{8}$ cup) dry white wine
200 ml (7 fl oz/$\frac{7}{8}$ cup) fish stock (broth)
2 shallots, skinned and chopped
75 g (3 oz/scant $\frac{1}{2}$ cup) crème fraîche (see page 10)
100 g (4 oz) sorrel leaves, trimmed
50 g (2 oz) butter
one 2 kg (4$\frac{1}{2}$ lb) salmon, skinned and filleted

1 Put the white wine, fish stock (broth) and shallots into a large saucepan and simmer until reduced to about 200 ml (7 fl oz/1 scant cup). Remove from the heat and incorporate the crème fraîche, then reduce by half again.
2 Add the sorrel leaves and gradually add 25 g (1 oz/2 tbsp) of the butter, stirring until the leaves soften and blend into the sauce. Keep warm over hot water.
3 Cut each salmon fillet into 3 pieces. Fry the salmon pieces in the remaining butter for 2 minutes on each side, over a brisk heat. Place in warm individual serving dishes and cover with the sauce.

MONKFISH IN LETTUCE PARCELS

For a summer dinner party alfresco, this dish makes a superb main course. Steamed inside a wrapping of lettuce leaves, the monkfish retains its firm texture, and the cucumber-and-wine sauce is sublime.

SERVES 6

225 g (8 oz/2 cups) button mushrooms
2 shallots, skinned and finely chopped
juice of 1 lemon
100 g (4 oz/$\frac{1}{2}$ cup) butter
1 large or 2 small soft lettuces
1 cucumber, peeled and seeded
200 ml (7 fl oz) white wine
10 ml (2 tsp) caster (superfine) sugar
salt and pepper
1.6 kg (3$\frac{1}{2}$ lb) monkfish, skinned and cut into 18 pieces
225 g (8 oz/1 cup) crème fraîche (see page 10)

1 Put the button mushrooms and chopped shallots into a saucepan. Sprinkle with the lemon juice, add 5 ml (1 tsp) of the butter and heat gently until most of the liquid evaporates.
2 Blanch the lettuce leaves in boiling water for 30 seconds. Cool them under cold running water. Dry on a clean cloth.
3 Purée half of the cucumber in a blender or food processor. Cut the remaining half into thin sticks.
4 Heat the white wine and cucumber purée in a pan and reduce to a glaze. Cook the remaining cucumber sticks in the rest of the butter, with a little sugar and salt and pepper to taste. Set aside.
5 Place each piece of fish on 1–2 lettuce leaves, allowing 3 parcels per person. Put some mushroom mixture on top and wrap the leaves around securely.
6 Secure the parcels with wooden cocktail sticks (toothpicks). Place in a steamer basket, cover tightly and steam over rapidly boiling water for 7–8 minutes.
7 Sieve the reduced cucumber sauce, add the crème fraîche and heat gently. Sprinkle the cucumber sticks over the parcels and coat with the sauce.

CHEESY CHICKEN IN FILO PASTRY

Cooked in this way, chicken breast meat remains succulent and tender, and the melted cheese is mouthwatering. A slice of avocado adds an exotic touch, and the aroma of fresh herbs wafts up as you cut into the golden filo parcel. Be sure to keep the pastry covered until you actually make the parcels; filo must not be allowed to dry out.

SERVES 4

4 chicken breasts, skinned and boned
1 ripe avocado, peeled, stoned (pitted) and sliced
8 slices of mozzarella cheese
8 sheets of filo pastry, each about 19 × 38 cm
($7\frac{1}{2}$ × 15 inches)
60 ml (4 tbsp) olive oil

small bunch of fresh herbs (such as tarragon, chives, marjoram), finely chopped
30 ml (2 tbsp) white wine
salt and pepper

1 Slice the chicken breasts almost in half horizontally, and insert 2 or 3 avocado slices inside. Place 2 slices of the mozzarella cheese on top of the avocado, then close the chicken breast.
2 Put each chicken breast on to 2 sheets of filo pastry lightly brushed with olive oil, then sprinkle each with the fresh herbs, 7.5 ml ($1\frac{1}{2}$ tsp) of the white wine and salt and pepper.
3 Wrap the filo around the chicken, tucking in the edges securely. Make 4 parcels. Brush the tops with oil and place on a baking sheet.
4 Bake at 200°C/400°F/mark 6 for 20–25 minutes until the filo pastry is golden and crisp, and the chicken cooked through.

SEAFOOD STIR-FRY WITH SAFFRON NOODLES

Saffron gives fish dishes a unique flavour, and here saffron noodles complement the stir-fried seafood and creamy sauce perfectly.

SERVES 8–10

900 g (2 lb) mussels, cleaned (see page 49)
450 g (1 lb) cod, filleted and skinned
450 g (1 lb) mackerel, filleted and skinned
450 g (1 lb) squid, cleaned
450 g (1 lb) frozen prawns (shrimp), thawed
75 ml (5 tbsp) olive oil
45 ml (3 tbsp) chopped fresh dill
1 garlic clove, skinned and crushed
150 ml ($\frac{1}{4}$ pint/$\frac{1}{3}$ cup) double (heavy) cream
350 g (12 oz) Chinese egg noodles
6 saffron strands
30 ml (2 tbsp) milk
25 g (1 oz/2 tbsp) butter

1 To steam the mussels open, place them in a large saucepan, cover tightly and cook over a medium-high heat for 5–7 minutes, shaking the pan from time to time. Remove the mussels from their shells, discarding any that have not opened.
2 Cut the cod and mackerel into small cubes. Slice the squid and dry the prawns (shrimp) on paper towels.
3 Heat the oil in a wok or large frying pan, and stir-fry the cod, mackerel and squid in it for 4–5 minutes until they begin to cook through. Add the dill and garlic and stir-fry for another 1–2 minutes.
4 Add the mussels and prawns and stir-fry for a further 2 minutes. Stir in the cream, mixing well. Set aside, covered with a lid, while preparing the noodles.
5 Cook the noodles in a saucepan of boiling, slightly salted water for about 3–4 minutes or until al dente. Soak the saffron threads in the milk, then toss the milk and saffron into the hot noodles with the butter.
6 Make a ring of noodles around the edge of a large, serving dish. Pile the seafood into the centre and serve. Alternatively, serve the noodles separately.

RIGHT: Seafood Stir-fry with Saffron Noodles (this page)

SALADS & SIDE DISHES

NOODLES WITH SPICY PEANUT BUTTER DRESSING

Chinese egg noodles make a delicious side dish, served warm and tossed in a spicy peanut butter dressing. Soft in texture yet with an intriguing "bite," this makes a perfect dish for a summer dinner party.

SERVES 6

350 g (12 oz) Chinese egg noodles
FOR THE SPICY PEANUT BUTTER DRESSING
30 ml (2 tbsp) crunchy peanut butter
15 ml (1 tbsp) soy sauce
5 ml (1 tsp) garam masala paste (see page 9)
60 ml (4 tbsp) dark sesame oil (see page 10)
3 spring onions (scallions), trimmed and finely sliced

1 To make the Spicy Peanut Butter Dressing, mix the peanut butter with the soy sauce and garam masala. Beat until smooth. Stir in the sesame oil, and beat until blended. Finally, fold in the spring onions (scallions).
2 Cook the noodles in boiling salted water for about 4–5 minutes, until just tender. Drain, and rinse the noodles under running warm water. Shake dry in a colander or sieve.
3 Put the noodles into a warm serving dish. Pour the dressing over the top and mix thoroughly.

SPICY SUMMER VEGETABLE SALAD

With freshly picked produce, the flavours of this salad are unbelievable. The spicy dressing suits the ingredients perfectly.

SERVES 4

1 large cauliflower, cut into florets
225 g (8 oz) new potatoes
175 g (6 oz) French (green) beans or yellow beans
175 g (6 oz) mangetout (snow peas), trimmed
1 large yellow pepper, seeded and quartered
8 radishes, thinly sliced (optional)
chopped fresh parsley
chopped fresh coriander
lettuce leaves
FOR THE SPICY DRESSING
100 g (4 oz/½ cup) fromage frais (see page 9)
45 ml (3 tbsp) Vinaigrette (see page 42)
2.5 ml (½ tsp) garam masala (see page 9)

1 To make the dressing, blend the fromage frais, Vinaigrette and garam masala together in a bowl. Leave to stand while preparing the vegetables.
2 Steam the potatoes for about 25 minutes, the beans for about 15 minutes, the cauliflower for about 10 minutes and the mangetout (snow peas) for about 5 minutes, until they are just tender or al dente.
3 Grill (broil) the pepper, skin side up, until soft. Peel off the skin, remove seeds and slice.
4 Thinly slice the cauliflower florets. Slice the mangetout into thin diagonal strips. Cut the French (green) beans in half crosswise. Combine with the radishes, parsley and coriander.
5 Mix the vegetables thoroughly with the dressing. Pile on to a platter lined with the lettuce leaves.
Illustrated on pages 126–7

I cannot see what flowers are at my feet,
Nor what soft incense hangs upon the boughs,
But, in embalmèd darkness, guess each sweet
Wherewith the seasonable month endows
The grass, the thicket, and the fruit-tree wild;
White hawthorn, and the pastoral eglantine;
Fast fading violets covered up in leaves;
And mid-May's eldest child,
The coming musk-rose, full of dewy wine,
The murmurous haunt of flies on summer eves.
John Keats: "Ode to a Nightingale"

GINGERY TOMATOES

In this exotic salad, ripe tomatoes are dressed in a spicy mixture that includes ginger and mustard.

SERVES 6

900 g (2 lb) ripe tomatoes
1 large crisp lettuce, shredded
FOR THE GINGER DRESSING
15 ml (1 tbsp) finely grated fresh ginger root
30 ml (2 tbsp) finely chopped spring onion (scallion)
15 ml (1 tbsp) finely chopped shallot
30 ml (2 tbsp) lemon juice
5 ml (1 tsp) Dijon mustard
50 ml (2 fl oz/$\frac{1}{4}$ cup) olive oil
salt and pepper

1 Mix all the dressing ingredients together in a screw-top jar and shake thoroughly. Leave for 30 minutes.
2 Pour boiling water over the tomatoes and leave for 1 minute. Peel off the skins and cut the flesh into small cubes. Drain in a colander for 20–30 minutes.
3 Toss the tomatoes in the Ginger Dressing. Heap them on to a bed of shredded lettuce in a serving dish.

GREEN SALAD WITH CHINESE DRESSING

Here, several different types of lettuce are enhanced by a distinctive Chinese-inspired dressing.

SERVES 6

1 Lollo Rosso (red leaf) lettuce, trimmed
1 crisp lettuce such as Webb's or iceberg, trimmed
hearts of 3 cos (romaine) lettuces
bunch of watercress, trimmed
FOR THE CHINESE DRESSING
20 ml (4 tsp) soy sauce
50 ml (2 fl oz) orange juice
1 garlic clove, skinned and crushed
1.8 cm ($\frac{3}{4}$ inch) piece fresh ginger root, peeled and grated
7.5 ml (1$\frac{1}{2}$ tsp) tarragon vinegar

1 To make the Chinese Dressing, combine all the dressing ingredients in a screw-top jar and shake vigorously. Leave to stand for at least 1 hour.
2 Put all the salad ingredients into a large salad bowl. Just before serving add the Chinese Dressing.

DESSERTS

CHILLED MELON DESSERT

This melon dish, in which the kirsch-flavoured fruit is mixed with sweetened fromage frais and served in the half-shells, makes a light, refreshing dessert.

SERVES 6

3 ogen (or cantaloupe) melons
45 ml (3 tbsp) kirsch
50 g (2 oz/$\frac{1}{2}$ cup) icing (confectioners') sugar, sifted
450 g (1 lb) fromage frais (see page 9)
elderflower sprays, to decorate

1 Cut the melons in half and scoop out all the seeds. Remove the flesh with a melon baller, or cut into small cubes, reserving the shells.
2 Put the melon into a bowl and sprinkle with the kirsch. Chill.
3 Stir the sugar into the fromage frais. Divide the melon among the half-shells. Mix in the sweetened fromage frais. Chill thoroughly before serving.

FLAMING PEACHES

The sight of these flambéed peaches is sensational as the dish is carried out into a darkening garden, on to a candlelit table. It makes a memorable finale to an alfresco dinner party.

SERVES 4

6 fresh peaches
40 g (1$\frac{1}{2}$ oz/$\frac{1}{3}$ cup) icing (confectioners') sugar
60 ml (4 tbsp) brandy
double (heavy) cream or sweetened crème fraîche
(see page 10), to serve

1 Cover the peaches with boiling water and leave for a few minutes, then peel them. Cut the peaches in half and remove the stones (pits). Slice the flesh.

2 Poach the peaches with a little water in a pan for 3 minutes. (Or microwave in a shallow dish with a little water for 1 minute.) Add the sugar and stir well.
3 Pour the brandy over the peaches, bring to the table and set alight. Serve at once, accompanied by thick cream or sweetened crème fraîche to pass around.

ELDERFLOWER ICE CREAM

Delicate flavours of the season to round off a relaxed dinner at dusk—an ice cream made with elderflowers and garnished with rose petals.

SERVES 6

450 ml ($\frac{3}{4}$ pint/2 cups) milk
6 heads of elderflowers
3 egg yolks
50 g (2 oz/$\frac{1}{4}$ cup) caster (superfine) sugar
25 g (1 oz/$\frac{1}{4}$ cup) plain (all-purpose) flour
300 ml ($\frac{1}{2}$ pint/1$\frac{1}{4}$ cups) double (heavy) cream
3 egg whites, stiffly beaten
rose petals, to decorate (optional)

1 Heat the milk in a saucepan to just below boiling point. Remove from the heat and add the elderflowers. Cover and leave to infuse for 10 minutes.
2 Beat the egg yolks with the sugar in a bowl until pale and creamy. Beat in the flour. Gradually mix in the hot, strained milk thoroughly.
3 Pour the mixture into a heavy-bottomed saucepan and stir over a very gentle heat until it thickens. Simmer for 5 minutes, then cool completely.
4 When cool, stir in the cream and fold in the stiffly beaten egg whites. Pour the mixture into a freezer container and freeze for at least 4 hours.
5 Soften the ice cream for 30 minutes at room temperature before serving. Remove the white "heel" from the rose petals, if using, then scatter over the top.

RIGHT: *Chilled Melon Dessert (this page)*

RASPBERRY ALMOND CRUNCH

The fleeting season of raspberries epitomizes high summer for me—their unique taste is never the same at any other time of the year, even though they freeze quite well. This simple dessert is made up of raspberries, browned flaked (slivered) almonds and crushed almond macaroons folded into crème fraîche. If possible, scatter some stock petals over the dish just before serving.

SERVES 6

900 g (2 lb) raspberries, hulls removed
icing (confectioners') sugar, to taste
100 g (4 oz/1 cup) flaked (slivered) almonds, chopped
and browned
100 g (4 oz/1 cup) small almond macaroons, crushed
450 ml ($\frac{3}{4}$ pint/2 cups) crème fraîche (see page 10)
stock petals, to decorate (optional)

1 Mix the raspberries with sugar to taste, and put to one side.
2 Fold the browned nuts and macaroons into the crème fraîche, then toss in the raspberries. Chill thoroughly.
3 If possible, decorate the dessert with a few stock petals just before serving.

RIGHT: *Raspberry Almond Crunch (this page)*

142

INDEX

Page numbers in *italics* indicate captions.

Almond cookies 64, *64*
Apple cake, Danish 67
Apricot layer, crunchy 122
Asparagus
  Asparagus soup with coriander *128*, 133
  Mangetout (snow pea) and avocado
    vinaigrette 133, *133*
Aubergine
  Chinese ratatouille 110
  Oriental pâté 38
  Spiced aubergine dip 83
  Vegetable kebabs 92, *92*
Avocado
  Cheesy chicken in filo pastry 135
  Mangetout (snow pea) and avocado
    vinaigrette 133, *133*

Bananas, melt-in-the-mouth 104
Basil bread, hot *92*, 133
Bass, Oriental steamed 112, *112*
Berries
  Berries with dried fruit 16
  Blackberry sorbet 54, *54*
  Blueberry lassi 28
  Frozen berry yogurt 19, *19*
  Individual summer puddings 52, *52*
  Melon with berries *16*, 19
  Raspberry almond crunch 142, *142*
Blackberry sorbet 54, *54*
Black currant shortcake 122
Blueberry lassi 28
Borage fruit cup with white wine 76
Bread
  All-American muffins 60, *63*
  English country house scones 63, *63*
  Hot basil bread *92*, 133
Bread dishes
  Cucumber sandwiches à la Ritz 60, *63*
  Eggs in pitta pockets 22
  Focaccia alla caprese 48, *48*
  Grilled (broiled) tomatoes on fried bread
    23, *23*
  Marinated mushroom kebabs 97
  Mushroom toasts with marjoram 22
Brownies, chocolate walnut 68
Buckwheat kedgeree 21

Caesar salad, jumbo 118
Cake, Danish apple 67
Carrot salad, Chinese 96, *97*
Cheese straws with sesame 85, *85*
Cheesy chicken in filo pastry 135
Cheesy tomatoes 96
Chervil soufflé-omelette 46
Chicken
  Cheesy chicken in filo pastry 135
  Chunky chicken patties 48
  Creamy ginger chicken 51, *51*
  Miniature chicken patties 48
Chicory (endive) and celery salad 44
Chinese carrot salad 96, *97*
Chinese ratatouille 110
Chocolate roulade 68, *68*
Chocolate walnut brownies 68
Cookies, almond 64, *64*
Corn on the cob, garlicky *93*, 102
Cucumber sandwiches à la Ritz 60, *63*
Cucumber soup, chilled 40, *40*

Danish apple cake 67
Desserts 52–5, 104, 122–5, 140–3
Dips
  Minty yogurt dip 86
  Oriental pâté 38
  Spiced aubergine (eggplant) dip 83
  Tzatziki with dill 38

Eel, smoked, scrambled eggs with 20
Eggplant *see* Aubergine
Eggs
  Chervil soufflé-omelette 46
  Eggs in pitta pockets 22
  Omelette primavera 114
  Picnic omelette fines herbes 49
  Scrambled eggs with smoked eel 20

Elderflower champagne 80
Elderflower ice cream 140
Endive and celery salad 44
Exotic refresco 32

Field mushrooms with marjoram 22
Filo pastry
  Cheesy chicken in filo pastry 135
  Filo party pieces 82
First courses 38–41, 130–3
Fish
  Barbecued salmon 92
  Buckwheat kedgeree 21
  Monkfish in lettuce parcels 134
  Oriental steamed bass 112, *112*
  Salmon with sorrel 134
  Seafood stir-fry with saffron noodles 136,
    136
  Smoked salmon rolls 130, *130*
  Tuna steaks with fennel 110
  see also Shellfish
Flageolets al pesto 96, *97*
Focaccia alla caprese 48, *48*
Fruit cup, tropical *25*, 28, *28*
Fruit dishes 16–19
  Barbecued pears 104
  Berries with dried fruit 16
  Blackberry sorbet 54, *54*
  Black currant shortcake 122
  Chilled melon dessert 140, *140*
  Creamy peach gâteau 70
  Crunchy apricot layer 122
  Danish apple cake 67
  Flaming peaches 140
  Fresh fruit salad 16
  Frozen berry yogurt 19, *19*
  Fruit salad on a stick 104
  Fruit with yogurt 19
  Golden grapefruit brûlée 16
  Golden pear tart 125, *125*
  Individual summer puddings 52, *52*
  Lemon tart 67, *67*
  Melon with berries *16*, 19
  Melt-in-the-mouth bananas 104
  Raspberry almond crunch 142, *142*
  Simple mango sorbet 122
  Strawberry jam 63, *63*
  Summer fruit bowl 19, *19*
  Sunshine fruit bowl 19, *19*
Fruit drinks
  Blueberry lassi 28
  Borage fruit cup with white wine 76
  Chilled wine-cup with mint 79
  Exotic refresco 32
  Lemon balm cup 32, *32*
  Mangoade 32
  Minted grape juice 31
  Peach shake 80, *80*
  Rosemary claret cup 76, *85*
  Tea punch 79, *79*
  Tropical fruit cup *25*, 28, *28*

Gâteau, creamy peach 70
Ginger chicken, creamy 51, *51*
Gingery tomatoes 139
Grape juice, minted 31
Grapefruit brûlée, golden 16
Green salad with Chinese dressing 139
Green salad with walnut-oil dressing 42
Guacamole tacos 82

Herbed olives 86

Ice cream
  Elderflower ice cream 140
  Light mint ice cream 52

Jam, strawberry 63, *63*

Kebabs
  Fruit salad on a stick 104
  Marinated mushroom kebabs 97
  Tangy shellfish *89*, 94
  Vegetable kebabs 92, *92*
Kedgeree, buckwheat 21

Lassi, blueberry 28
Leeks in blue-cheese dressing 102
Lemon balm cup 32, *32*
Lemon tart 67, *67*

Main dishes
  Barbecue 92–4
  Breakfast 20–3
  Dinner 134–7
  Lunch 46–51
  Supper 110–14
Mangetout
  Mangetout and avocado vinaigrette 133,
    133
  Mangetout and new potato salad 44
  Rice noodles with summer vegetables
    116
  Spicy summer vegetable salad *127*, 138
Mango
  Mangoade 32
  Simple mango sorbet 122
Mayonnaise
  Homemade mayonnaise 101
  Raspberry vinegar mayonnaise 44
  Sesame seed mayonnaise 101
  Tahini mayonnaise 100
  Watercress mayonnaise 94
Melon
  Chilled melon dessert 140, *140*
  Melon with berries *16*, 19
Mint ice cream, light 52
Mint julep 79, *79*
Mint tea, chilled 28
Minted grape juice 31
Minty yogurt dip 86
Mixed salad with tahini mayonnaise 100
Monkfish in lettuce parcels 134
Muffins, all-American 60, *63*
Mushrooms
  Marinated mushroom kebabs 97
  Mushroom toasts with marjoram 22
  Ruchetta ai funghi 116, *116*
  Vegetable kebabs 92, *92*
Mussels and pasta twists with basil 49

Nibbles 82–7
Noodles *see* Pasta

Oat and sesame crunch 64
Olives, herbed 86
Omelettes
  Chervil soufflé-omelette 46
  Omelette primavera 114
  Picnic omelette fines herbes 49
Oriental pâté 38
Oriental steamed bass 112, *112*

Pasta
  Mussels and pasta twists with basil 49
  Noodles with spicy peanut butter
    dressing 138
  Pasta salad with basil and cheese 45, *127*
  Rice noodles with summer vegetables
    116
  Seafood stir-fry with saffron noodles 136,
    136
  Tagliatelle with fennel 46
Pâté, Oriental 38
Peaches
  Creamy peach gâteau 70
  Flaming peaches 140
  Peach shake 80, *80*
Pears
  Barbecued pears 104
  Golden pear tart 125, *125*
Pepper and rice salad 42
Picnic omelette fines herbes 49
Potatoes, new
  Mangetout (snow peas) and new potato
    salad 44
  Omelette primavera 114
  Spicy summer vegetable salad *127*, 138
Prawns *see* Shellfish
Provençal stuffed tomatoes 44

Radicchio, hot, Italian style 119, *119*
Raspberry almond crunch 142, *142*
Raspberry sauce 52
Ratatouille, Chinese 110
Rice noodles with summer vegetables
  116
Rice salad, pepper and 42
Rose cordial 31
Rosemary claret cup 76, *85*
Ruchetta ai funghi 116, *116*

Salad dressings
  Black bean dressing 96
  Blue cheese dressing 102
  Blue cheese and yogurt dressing 100
  Chinese dressing 139
  Garlic vinaigrette 118
  Ginger dressing 139
  Lemony yogurt dressing 118
  Orange and ginger dressing 44
  Sesame oil dressing 119
  Spicy dressing 138
  Spicy peanut butter dressing 138
  Vinaigrette 42
  Walnut oil dressing 42
  see also Mayonnaise
Salade noisette 118
Salads 42–5, 96–102, 118–21, 138–9
Salmon
  Barbecued salmon 92
  Salmon with sorrel 134
  Smoked salmon rolls 130, *130*
Sandwiches, cucumber, à la Ritz 60, *63*
Sauces
  Béchamel 49
  Raspberry sauce 52
  Strawberry sauce 20
Scones, English country house 63, *63*
Scrambled eggs with smoked eel 20
Seafood stir-fry with saffron noodles 136,
  136
Sesame cheese crumbles 82
Shellfish
  Mussels and pasta twists with basil 49
  Seafood stir-fry with saffron noodles 136,
    136
  Tangy shellfish *89*, 94
Shortcake, black currant 122
Side dishes 44, 96–102, 116–17, 138
Smoked salmon rolls 130, *130*
Snow peas *see* Mangetout
Sorbets
  Blackberry sorbet 54, *54*
  Simple mango sorbet 122
Soufflé-omelette, chervil 46
Soups
  Asparagus soup with coriander *128*, 133
  Chilled cucumber soup 40, *40*
Spicy summer vegetable salad *127*, 138
Starters *see* First courses
Strawberry jam 63, *63*
Strawberry sauce 20
Summer fruit bowl 19, *19*
Summer puddings, individual 52, *52*
Sunshine fruit bowl 19, *19*

Tacos, guacamole 82
Tagliatelle with fennel 46
Tarts
  Golden pear tart 125, *125*
  Lemon tart 67, *67*
Tea, chilled mint 28
Tea punch 79, *79*
Tomatoes
  Cheesy tomatoes 96
  Focaccia alla caprese 48, *48*
  Gingery tomatoes 139
  Grilled (broiled) tomatoes on fried bread
    23, *23*
  Provençal stuffed tomatoes 44
  Tomato salad with tarragon *51*, 119
  Tomatoes with blue cheese and yogurt
    dressing 100
Tossed salad with sesame seed mayonnaise
  101
Tropical fruit cup *25*, 28, *28*
Tuna steaks with fennel 110
Tzatziki with dill 38

Vegetable kebabs 92, *92*
Vinaigrette 42
  Garlic Vinaigrette 118

Waffles, hot, with strawberry sauce 20
Wine cups 76, 79, *85*

Yogurt
  Frozen berry yogurt 19, *19*
  Fruit with yogurt 19
  Minty yogurt dip 86
  Tzatziki with dill 38